The Art of Starting Again

A Poweful Guide to Goal Setting and Visualisation

GETTING OUT OF THE FUNK, SURVIVING LIFE
CHANGES AND PLANNING FOR
A BRIGHTER FUTURE

Andrea Bibby

Published 2024 by Urban Viking
©Andrea Bibby 2024.

Images & graphic designs ©Andrea Bibby 2024

www.urbanviking.tv

Disclaimer:

The information and opinions contained in this book are a friendly take on issues from the author's own life and experience. All circumstances are different. The reader should seek professional advice relevant to their own needs if they identify with any of the challenging issues raised.

To anybody who is experiencing a difficult time. I have written this book for you; to get you through and support you as you elevate. Never be afraid to start again. To become liberated from all that is holding you back is the power you give to yourself to take control of your own destiny. Right or wrong, this is your path. The only things you regret are the ones you didn't do.

To anyone out there who is struggling with their feelings right now. If this book can prevent one death through suicide or domestic abuse, or stop one family from suffering the trauma of violence, then I have done something worthwhile. Always reach out.

To every soul who has taught me to become who I am. I am grateful for the lessons and the blessings that have come into my life. Even the ugly ones!

This is the book I wish I had through my earliest dark times. I continue to use the wisdom gained and will be forever building more insight

Keep up to date with my latest publications at www.urbanviking.tv.

"When things go wrong,
don't go with them."

- Elvis Presley

"I am not what happened to me...
I am what I choose to become."

- Carl Jung

Contents

I am, and always will be, a work in progress.

Introduction

This Book is my gift to others, who feel the need for change in their lives. I devised a rudimental version of this self-help guide, in the depths of my own despair. I was rock bottom, in an on-off abusive relationship with no money, piles of debt, confused, already had been married twice, with four children. I was a single parent with no family around me, living on the other side of the world from everyone who knew me well. The relationship had left me isolated and vulnerable with few resources to call upon. I'd formed unhealthy habits as a way of coping in the situation and I was feeling very low. So low, that if I sank any further, I felt like a hole was going to swallow me up. So much about my life had to change.

I thought about my life, and all the parts of it that I could imagine - I found eight; eight areas of my life, which all needed addressing. I thought about who I wanted to be in five years' time. I drew what I wanted to look like. This was at least ten years ago. I still haven't achieved all of those goals completely and, some have changed a little. I am still on track and that is okay. I have achieved many other goals in that time. I've written and published books, released music, gained confidence, ran music events, learned many new skills, completed a master's degree, and started my own company. Best of all, I found out who I am as a person.

Through it all, I managed to keep my head, always believing in the power of my mind to stop me from getting depressed. There were always times when things got very difficult; I had to ride a wave of situational depression, hold space, and survive.

Relationship endings are never easy; a minimum of three months with a massive hole in your life, bills, and other challenges. Life does not stop for you to heal, when you really need it to in so many ways. I have had to steer my brain through the fog on autopilot; achieving one small thing at a time, with my eye on the goal of who I needed to be, while at the same time, allowing myself to feel those awful feelings, and practice self-care.

At the time of drafting this book, I was actually in another abusive relationship, and having to follow my own words as I wrote them, using my past as inspiration to survive this round of pain. Still, nothing prepares you for the upheaval. Each challenge is different, requiring different techniques to cope. It certainly doesn't get any easier the more you go through it. I was trying to survive long enough to stand on my own two feet, and get out under my own terms. This was not to be. The abuse escalated and the stranglehold was intolerable, leaving me no choice, other than to say, "you need to get help, or one of us has to go." With that, my partner proceeded an eight-week reign of terror, which ended in a court order and a criminal conviction. Dealing with the pressure of the breakdown was exacerbated by the feelings of rejection, and emotional torture.

When this kind of fog and trauma is affecting you, it may not be the right time to set a lot of goals. It can help you, as part of self-care, to visualise yourself in brighter days; to design a new image, plan to do one thing you enjoy in a day - and do it - even if you do not feel like it.

The power of autopilot has seen me through some very hard times. With the achievement of one small thing a day; a phone call, a form, a meal, a bath, I have found myself a lot further along in dealing with things, than I would have been if I had waited until I was ready for the onslaught. Not getting angry or disappointed with loved ones when they do not understand, and showing gratitude for their well-meaning (often unhelpful) comments, will also stand you in good stead for when you get your brain back! You cannot always expect those close to you to understand if they have not been where you are. It is not their fault.

My approach in this book is about survival, focus and progress. Self-actualisation is still an ever-changing act of development. If we reach for the stars and fall short, we have still progressed. If we never strive, there is no growth. Things don't change if things don't change. If you do not visualise a positive future, things are never likely to be in your control. Managing and remaining in the present, and letting go of the past, are paramount in accessing a positive future.

Being adaptable and reviewing the goals every so often has helped me. Life always throws elements in that you can't control, or you may find you accept a curve ball, which alters the trajectory of your path. The most important thing is to retain focus by regular reviews on how you are feeling. I have never set a review timescale for my goal setting; however, I do notice that when I am feeling down, I review my current location on my pathway, and invariably find I have strayed.

The Art of Starting Again

IS DRIVEN BY YOUR FEELINGS

Prevention is better than cure, so if you are the type of person who is driven by time and order, then setting a date for reviewing your goals, is always a plus. You are more likely to get where you want to be faster, if you revisit at regular intervals. I would recommend no more than every three months for a full review. Daily, weekly, and monthly targets are ones we get to review accordingly.

There are many time-management and planning apps, or programs for your phone and computer available. I will not be looking at those in this book, as I want to keep focus on inspiring and motivating simple, powerful change with minimal barriers to doing so. This accessible method can be done when technology is part of the 'noise.' I explore some techniques for visualisation and manifesting a brighter future and activities to transform your limiting beliefs.

It is often best to turn off all technology, and be still, to feel what you want to do. To be undisturbed and even get out into nature, maybe visit your favourite thinking place, or just lock all the doors and switch off/unplug the phone. Just you, pen, and paper. This is self-care; so, try to find a space where you will not be interrupted. Perhaps toddler's naptime, or when everyone else is asleep or out. I invite you to take the time, for you.

One of the major forms of stress, is being out of control of your own life. You are the master of your own destiny. This life is not a dress rehearsal. Owning your direction, even if all feels hopeless, or if it is impossible right now, you can still plan for that to change and bide your time. Be secure in the knowledge that whatever you are going through will pass, the sun will set on this day and the sun will rise on a new day tomorrow – bringing new opportunities and fresh light. This is my way of coping in the face of adversity. Taking the time to heal your life and giving yourself hope every now and again, is the most valuable gift you can give to yourself. *The Art of Starting Again*, meets you where you are on your journey, from rock-bottom to self-actualisation, and enables you to select the elements from the book that will help you to move forward.

I bravely used the word 'powerful' in the title. The power lies in the simplicity of the method. All you need is a pen and a few pieces of A4 paper - no printer, no photocopies. These days, I quite often find myself doing this on the 'notes' app on my phone at bedtime. Whatever you can lay your hands on, and whatever works for you is the way forward.

I wish you the best outcome on your journey of elevation - Namaste.

Andrea

x

1

"Things don't change,
if things don't change."

I draw much inspiration from literature. One thing that has stood me in good stead over the years is the presence of various phrases. One that always comes to mind is the Serenity Prayer –

Reinhold Niebuhr, An American theologian wrote a prayer in the nineteen-fifties. It is often shortened to this:

"God, grant me the serenity to accept the things I cannot change,
Courage to change the things I can,
And wisdom to know the difference."

My method of planning and visualisation incorporates this into the philosophy. In order to be in control of life, as far as possible, you have to know your limits and work with them.

Creating change starts with changing one thing, one habit, consistently every day. We get to change the things we can control and work to grow our reality to match our vision. Our circle and our surroundings are a mirror of our beliefs. If we change our belief, we get to take steps to change our reality.

Things Don't Change if Things Don't Change

by Andrea Bibby

You train people how to treat you,
You can't make people like you,
You can't change someone - so what do you do?
Stop apologising and just be you.

If you don't know what to do - do nothing,
The right door will open at the right time,
You just have to keep knocking,
Trust in yourself, and you will be fine.

If you lie with dogs, you get fleas,
You can ask for things you don't deserve,
You can't make a silk purse out of a sows ear,
And you can't polish a turd!

Accept the things you cannot change,
And change the things you can,
You cannot please everyone,
So please yourself - make a stand.

This poem is a mash-up of lots of phrases I have developed from many sources over the years, and forms the rules that I try to live by.

15

Another favourite phrase of mine is, "If life gives you lemons, make lemonade." This phrase originates from Elbert Hubbard, an American Writer in an obituary he wrote for dwarf actor, Marshall Pinckney Wilder, in 1915. These phrases together demonstrate positivity in the face of adversity, and the idea of a realistic approach to what happens next.

The King of Jesters, was the title of the piece in which Hubbard gives praise to the actor, for his attitude and achievements, in the face of adversity.

"He was a walking refutation of that dogmatic statement, Mens sana in corpore sano. His was a sound mind in an unsound body. He proved the eternal paradox of things. He cashed in on his disabilities. He picked up the lemons that Fate had sent him and started a lemonade stand."

The phrase became a well-used, and well-known analogy for making the best of what you have been given. There are reasons to do things, and excuses not to do things. **If you find your *why*, your excuses will be meaningless.**

"When life gives you lemons, make lemonade."

2
Be kind to yourself

You listen to yourself more than you listen to anyone else.

Choose your words wisely.

You are blessed to be able to have this new beginning, starting with you, and where you are right now. You are invited to plan for a brighter future. You get to live with your past choices in peace and forgiveness, as you have this opportunity to learn to forgive yourself for those past choices, that you perhaps would choose differently now. Hindsight is a wonderful thing. Anybody who criticises the decisions you have made, probably did not know what the alternative was at the time, so you only need to reconcile with your own conscience.

Throughout this book, I'd like to offer a whistle-stop tour of some concepts that have drifted my way through various courses, therapies, and training opportunities, particularly in the fields of psychology and counselling. I will not go into too much depth, or detail. There are many more cognitive and learning theories, which help form changes in behaviour. I encourage you to do research in the areas that you feel called to investigate, if you would like to further your understanding. For some of you, this will be revision and connecting the dots. I have outlined things I have found interesting and useful, and hope you do too.

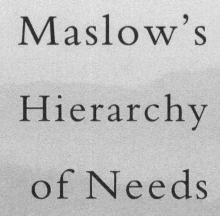

Maslow's Hierarchy of Needs

Self-Actualisation

Esteem

Social

Safety

Physiological

urbanviking.tv

Abraham Maslow, was a psychological theorist who created a pyramid diagram called *The Hierarchy of Needs,* which he first introduced in his 1943 paper, *A Theory of Human Motivation.* It describes how each level of human function depends on another being in place.

The bottom, or base layer refers to **Physiological** needs such as food, shelter, water, sex-drive, and good health.

Safety pertains to the need for not feeling threat. Order and organisation can help you feel safe, aside from physical safety, or the absence of verbal and emotional abuse.

Social requirements such as feeling loved, and like you belong come next, such as family ties, friendships, and relationships.

Having **self-esteem** means feeling good about achievements, and like you are worth something. Hearing positive statements from others and believing in your worth, is important for this to develop.

Self-actualisation refers to the appreciation of art and beauty in nature, spiritual satisfaction, and learning new things. Some people never self-actualise.

Life Stresses

1-10

1. DEATH OF A SPOUSE
2. DIVORCE
3. MARITAL SEPARATION
4. JAIL TERM
5. DEATH OF A CLOSE FAMILY MEMBER
6. PERSONAL INJURY OR ILLNESS
7. MARRIAGE
8. FIRED AT WORK
9. MARITAL RECONCILIATION
10. RETIREMENT

11-20

11. Change in health of a family member
12. Pregnancy
13. Sex difficulties
14. Gain of a new family member
15. Business readjustment
16. Change in financial state
17. Death of a close friend
18. Change to a different line of work
19. Change in number of arguments with a spouse
20. High Mortgage

21-32

21. Foreclosure of mortgage or loan
22. Change in work responsibilities
23. Son or daughter leaving home
24. Trouble with the in-laws
25. Outstanding personal achievement
26. Spouse begins or stops work
27. Start or end of school years
28. Change in living conditions
29. Revision of personal habits
30. Trouble with the boss
31. Change in work hours/conditions
32. Change in residence

33-43

33. Change in schools
34. Change in recreation
35. Change in religious activities
36. Change in social activities
37. Small mortgage
38. Change in sleeping habits
39. Change in number of family get-togethers
40. Change in eating habits
41. Vacation
42. Christmas
43. Minor violations of the law

An adaptation of the life-stress ranking as part of the 'social readjustment scale' by Holmes and Rahe
Adapted from Psychology: The Science of Mind and Behavior
by Richard D. Gross (1990) Hodder & Stoughton

Holmes and Rahe created a *social readjustment scale,* which ranked the most stressful events in a person's life. Those who experience a high score on this scale, with perhaps several events occurring in the space of a year, are said to be of higher risk of mental illness. It is not a given that mental illness occurs. I invite you to look at what has been happening for you. It can be useful to see where your life events sit in the rankings. Are you justified in feeling down or beaten?

This scale was drawn up many years ago, long before the internet and social media became part of daily life. More stress has been created by the fast pace of technological advancement, causing changes in human capacity to cope. I also see teenagers with an apparently higher rate of mental health issues. An awareness of these issues is enhanced by all this access to information. Social media has incited changes in social expectations and an ease of coming together without travel. This has had positive and negative effects on us all.

"There are no unthinkable thoughts and no unfeelable feelings"

This is a quote I have heard from many therapists. Whatever you are feeling, it is okay to feel that way. You can process that feeling when you are ready. Allow yourself to feel that feeling and say to yourself, "I accept this feeling." Whatever you are feeling right now, it is just fine to sit with it for a little while. It is about being mindful of the way you feel, checking-in on yourself and still being okay.

it's okay to feel

your feelings

3

The Window of Tolerance

The window of tolerance is a state of being. In a nutshell, feeling normal, calm, settled, and connected, makes for better relationships with others. In this state, you are able to self-regulate your emotions and calm yourself down when things are a little difficult. Some people seem to have a wide window of tolerance, because they might have learned some skill in dialling it down when things get too crazy, or have developed a way to recover from feelings of depression fairly succinctly. I would go so far as to say, taking time for healing can bring you back into this window, by setting good boundaries, and using some of the techniques I have outlined in this chapter, and throughout the book.

Living our whole lives, in the centre of this window of tolerance would be amazing, perhaps maybe a little dull at times. Dull is not necessarily a bad thing. The old phrase, "what goes up must come down," is so very true. Balance and order in any action, mitigates the intensity of an equal and opposite reaction. Excitement, adventure, and impulsivity can come at a cost, sometimes much bigger than expected. Striking a balance between calculated risks, and doing nothing with your life, is a tough call. A 'pros and cons' list can be very useful to help you consider life changes.

Sometimes life throws you a curve ball, meaning you may experience one, several, or other of the life-stresses identified earlier. If a person is not equipped to deal with trauma, then it could send them outside of the window of tolerance; either into 'fight or flight' response or into a 'freeze response.' In extreme cases, the freeze response can be utterly paralysing. Be wary of responding to stress with thrill-seeking or destructive behaviours, as these can become addictions.

Below is a link to a superb article by Lori Gill, RP, MACP, about the concept of the window of tolerance, a phrase coined by Dr. Dan Siegel around 1999. This is an extremely useful tool to have in your survival kit. The 'window of tolerance' has been used by therapists and organisations to help people heal from events in their lives. Using the illustration by Dezelic & Associates (2017) from the article, I have outlined how it works.

https://www.attachment-and-trauma-treatment-centre-for-healing.com/blogs/understanding-and-working-with-the-window-of-tolerance

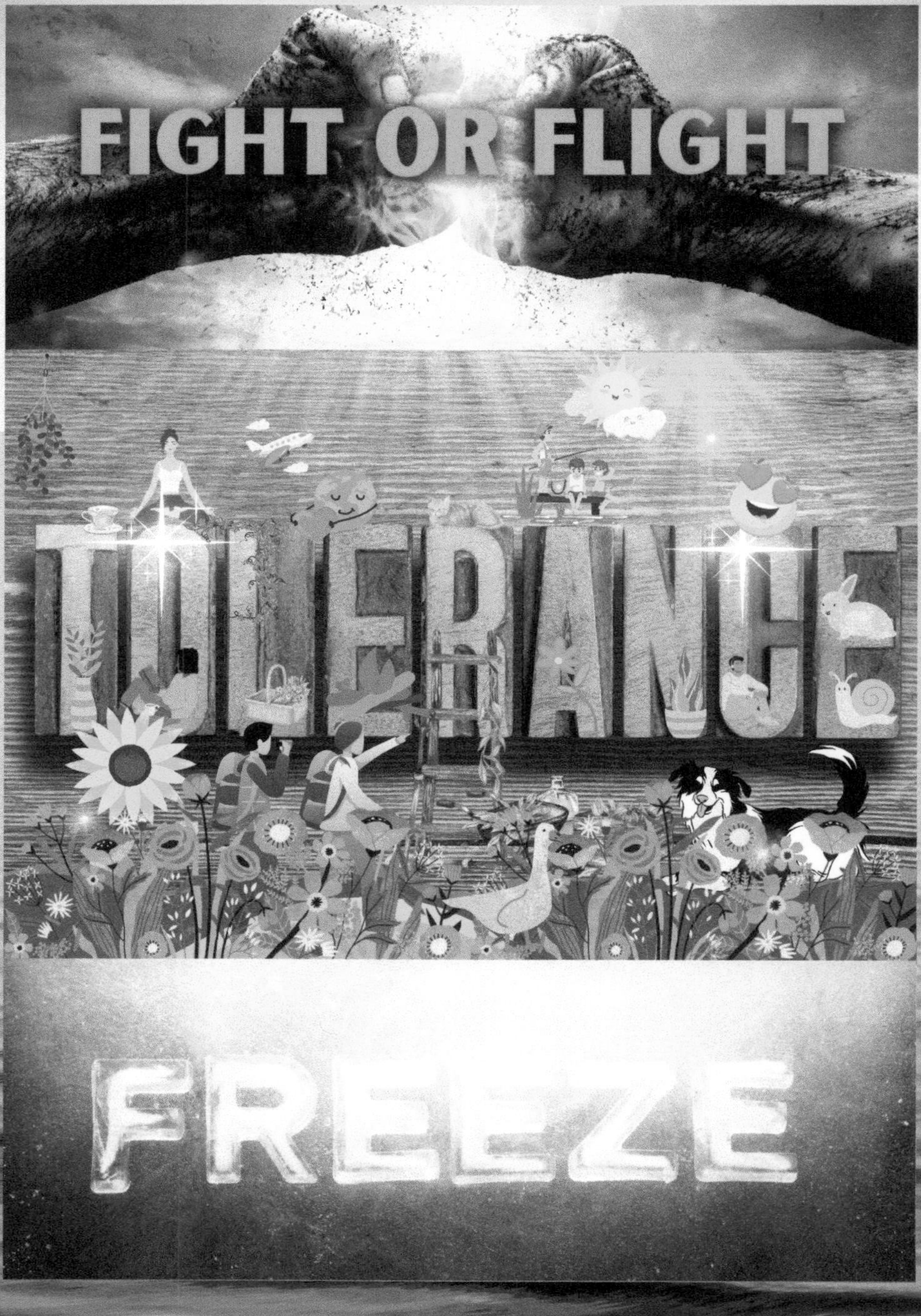
FIGHT OR FLIGHT
TOLERANCE
FREEZE

The window of tolerance, can explain personality quirks, pet hates, and even the reactions of people who measure highly on the Autistic Spectrum. To some people, hypersensitivity to things in their environment, cause intense discomfort and a traumatic response, as they are taken outside of their window of tolerance by such stimulus.

The window is a little bit like a comfort zone. I would suggest a comfort zone would be a band across the middle of the window of tolerance. Sometimes referred to as 'green brain,' the comfort zone is where we want to be. Above and below this comfort zone is what is tolerated as mild threat, discomfort or rather irritating, like a buffer zone, this is called the 'yellow brain,' according to *The Stoplight Approach International Association*. When we find ourselves in chaos or unable to cope, this is sometimes called 'red brain.'

You can read more about the Stoplight Approach here:

https://www.thestoplightapproach.org/our-philosophy

According to this article, when we are in 'yellow brain,' or outside of our comfort zone, we are only able to access 75% of our IQ.

In the 'red brain' moments, we are in fight or flight, or freeze mode. I identify times like this as 'when time stands still.' There is a section in the book about coping during such times.

The theory seems to be that once you experience being outside of this window of tolerance, your window of tolerance narrows. This explains how people with unresolved issues can go from feeling fine, to extremely depressed, or explosive in a short space of time.

We can widen the window of tolerance in several ways:

• Calming activities (craft, art, music, hobbies)
• Recovering from addiction
• Change limiting beliefs using mantras and positive statements
• Grounding and breathing exercises
• Mindfulness
• Make new choices

The fight or flight response, or 'hyper-arousal,' might look like a variety of these:

• Anxiety
• Overwhelmed
• Chaotic responses
• Outbursts (emotional or aggressive)
• Anger, aggression, or rage
• Rigidness
• Obsessive-compulsive behaviour, or thoughts
• Overeating/restricting
• Addictions
• Impulsivity

The freeze response, or 'hypo-arousal,' might look like a variety of these:

• Feign death response
• Disassociation
• Not Present
• Unavailable/shutdown
• Memory loss
• Disconnected
• Autopilot
• No display of emotion/flat
• Separation from self/feelings and emotions

All stress is relative to people's experiences, therefore each person will have a different tolerance level. Every journey is a deeply personal one. Developing empathy for others goes a long way to helping each other get by in life.

The cause of tipping out of the window of tolerance, is mainly due to our own fears:

- Unconscious thoughts
- Bodily feelings
- Control or lack of control
- Feeling unsafe
- "I do not exist"
- Abandonment
- Rejection

These tend to be trauma-related triggers, due to core beliefs about the 'self.' This is when 'emotional and physiological dysregulation' occurs. You can pull it back by slow deep breathing, and other 'widening' activities described previously.

An extreme and immediate example of being outside of the window of tolerance is hyperventilation or, a panic attack.

What causes fear?

Legitimate fears arise when we do not have control, or perceive that we do not have control of a situation. Coercion and threats from another person cause fear. Stalking, manipulation, and physical violence also cause fear, and with good reason. Empowerment of ourselves, is the key to gaining control, and that invariably comes with information. Knowledge is power.

Fear can also be the child within, or the person we have been in situations where something bad has happened. This inner child, or egoic manifestation of our past, is working to protect us.

Sometimes fear can arise regarding positive events, such as starting a YouTube Channel, or attending a concert. The voice of our parents could be echoing, "You need to get a real job," or "who wants to listen to you?" - It could be the excuses you make for not going out.

These feelings of shame, pain, discontent, or past failures, are working to look after our best interests in a misguided and limiting way, based on misconceptions, experience, or what we have been told.

There is a section in this book about tackling your limiting beliefs (page 84) in order help you to move on from this kind of fear.

Anxious? Free youself from limiting beliefs and fears

When you feel fear, yet know it is right that you do something, or go somewhere, why not thank your past self -your inner child, for their protection?

Sometimes we are sabotaged by a fear or memory where our inner child just wants to nurture and protect ourselves due to limiting fears from the past. Issues placed upon us that no longer serve our highest good can halt our ability to achieve.

we are blessed to be able to feel the fear, and do it anyway, in order to get ahead and achieve success. The best thing to do, in this situation, is to just start.

Feelings follow behaviour.

The age-old remedy of fresh air and sunshine can help widen the window of tolerance.

4

Panic Attacks

At sixteen years old I was a young mother. I was happy, yet the weight of the world was on my shoulders. Every small thing would stress me out and cause me to panic. Watching casualty, anything with mild threat, even crossing the road caused me to feel overwhelmed. It had something to do with the fact that one of the boys I knew growing up, from the local church, had passed away after being hit by a car, so it was perfectly acceptable that I should feel a little fragile.

I told my GP about the feelings I was having; she said I had post-natal depression, and prescribed me some bright red anti-depressants. I got home and looked at the bottle. My gut feeling told me this was wrong. I called a friend who warned me of the addictive nature of these tablets and how they make you feel empty. My friend, who had been on them after a bereavement, said that coming off them was very difficult and had to be reduced to a quarter of a tablet at the time. I disposed of the tablets and decided to seek an alternative solution.

I made an appointment with a different doctor, who told me that I was suffering from hyperventilation. This was a simple thing to deal with, and involved no medication. He informed me that it was all to do with taking in too much oxygen, which made me feel breathless, resulting in taking in even more air. So, the spiral continued until I was dizzy, feeling sick, and my breathing extremely out of control. Again leading to more panic to add fuel to the fire. This new doctor told me to breathe into a paper bag, and this would settle my breathing down. Needless to say, that once I understood what was happening physiologically, I was able to control my thoughts more, and the panic attacks stopped. In the absence of a paper bag, I would simply cup my hands.

Over the last two years, I have focused on self-healing and breathing exercises. I make it my business to go somewhere, even if I am sat in the car with my dog, and take a few minutes to have some deep breaths. I often record this for social media. It takes three good, deep breaths, to change the way your body is responding to the environment. Pranayama, or the art of breathing, is a feature of yoga, Reiki and meditation. These healing modalities have helped me avoid pain medication and assist me to sleep. Breath is life, control your breathing through practice, and you will control your life.

Pranayama or yogic is the preferred mode of elevation for many a recovering addict, and can help control breathing to avoid panic attacks. There are thousands of videos on YouTube to access, on breath work, pranayama and Yoga. I particularly admire Michael Bijker. My own content is expanding in this area online.

Here I wish to give you a quick survival breathing exercise for mindfulness. Focusing on the breath, can help us to remove focus on the stressful issues, so that we can be in control again.

Ocean Breath (Conquerer's breath) Ujjayi Pranayama

Step one, inhale through the nose exhale through the mouth.
inhale 4 seconds
exhale 8 seconds

Step two, inhale through the nose exhale through the nose.
inhale 4 seconds
exhale 8 seconds

You can adjust the length of the inward breath to suit your ability, keeping the ratio at 1:2

Sitting up straight, shoulders and face relaxed, eyes open or closed, whichever is easier for you. Have a quiet moment breathing normally, feel your mind and body relaxing.

Breathe in deeply through your nose. Exhaling slowly, make a long, gentle HA sound. Do this flow of breath for a few minutes, focus on the air traveling via the throat and out of the mouth.

Once used to the flow, we can begin Ujjayi breathing: With the mouth closed, repeat the same flow as described above. As you exhale through the nose, you will notice the sound of the ocean, as the breath flows along the back of the throat.

For beginners, it is best to limit this practice to five minutes. The ratio of the breath should ideally be 1:2.

A helpful website for young people is https://www.teenbreathe.co.uk

5

Addictions and Recovery

So, you managed to get hooked on the crutch? Sex, drugs, rock 'n' roll, cigarettes, and alcohol? All of the above? Risk-taking behaviours are stimulating, replacing that feeling of danger or lack of control. The trauma still owns you, if you are replacing one maladaptive drama for another. It may feel edgy and cool, in reality – it's still being fucked up. It causes you to be attractive to rescuers, or equally fucked up individuals. I'm not one to judge. Elevation is key. Of circle, of habits, of finances, of health, of all areas in life. It all starts with your consistent action.

I can identify certain crutches, or maladaptive behaviours, that have been my 'go-to' solutions for stress. Some people come to experience this on a grand scale, and become addicted to substances, creating a further problem and, again, narrowing the window of tolerance. Ideally, our higher selves would invite us to start with therapy, yoga, breathing, healing, and natural therapies, before reaching for the drink, drugs, cigarettes, sex, chocolate, or seeking approval from the opposite sex on your mobile phone. Can we simply nip it in the bud? Unfortunately, to access therapy, we have to be ready to listen, and talk about our issues, which is often painful and emotional. We also have to be able to reason with the devil on our shoulder, the one that speaks louder than our higher self. The one who rushes us off to the familiar place of fear, danger, and being out of control. We are used to that, we know how it feels.

I tried 'Better Help' online therapy. It cost money, which we don't all have access to. I had around seven 'sessions.' I was facing some painful truths about my relationship and myself. I was overeating, and putting up with a devastating lack of control in my life, having been told that I couldn't go home, after travelling to a distant land, by my husband. This left me with the choice of breaking up the family or living somewhere I didn't want to be.

I didn't want the marriage to be over, I wanted to get better. I wasn't ready for the therapy, I was dealing with surviving in the situation and therapy seemed like a luxury. I left him eventually, and in my attempts to move forward with life, the children developed a few issues of their own, and life went from bad to worse in the year that followed. So, I cut my losses and took my children back to my hometown, to the family. My gut instinct was telling me to go home three years before. I hadn't, yet, had a 'gutful.'

I should follow my own advice! As the saying goes, "you can't see the woods for the trees." This is so true when you are stuck in a situation, surviving; yet others can see where you need to go. You can't see your way out, so you battle some more.

Organisations like Women's Aid and Rehabilitation Centres understand the journey is not straightforward. You might lose friends because they get frustrated. This is because they care. Your toxic situation begins to affect their wellbeing, and the best thing they can do, after trying to tell you over and over, is to step to one side and let you find out the hard way. These organisations will take you back, over, and over, and this is a true lifesaver in the end. Best going to them as well as keeping your friends, knowing when to be strong in your own resolve, and when to follow advice is a tough call. Not everyone will understand your journey but 'those that mind don't matter, and the ones that matter don't mind.'

The way I see an addiction is; anything that negatively affects your health (immediate or long term), behaviour, finances and relationships, but you keep doing it anyway. Every time you do it, you risk more and more. This is not being dramatic. This is the stuff most people know!!!

• Consistently eating eight chocolate bars a day can lead to Type II Diabetes.

• Smoking regularly can make you ill, poor and smell awful.

• Smoking pot, taking recreational drugs and some prescription medications can lead to serious poverty, mood swings, inability to think straight, and paranoia.

• Drinking can pickle your organs, destroy your brain cells and ruin lives.

I will not go on, as the list is endless. The best thing to do, is not to start. If you catch yourself doing without food to pay for cigarettes and alcohol, it is an addiction. If you find yourself being moody with your kids because some guy is talking to you on the internet, it is a problem. If your bills are not paid, yet you are buying the latest trainers at three times the cost of your phone bill, to make you feel better, then that is destructive. Before long, these things are controlling you. I would go as far as to say, the behaviours I have listed, and more, are coping mechanisms for when you are outside of your window of tolerance, or replacement risk-taking behaviours for our trauma. Finding healthy, constructive alternatives is key, as is getting the right supporting organisation behind you. You can do it.

This is just a short list of ideas. I'd suggest identifying a certain behaviour that you would like to stop doing. You could list at least five alternatives and create a reduction plan. Focusing on alternatives, barriers, and limits. It can be helpful to watch inspiring videos on YouTube. Imagine what people see when they see you now. Were you always this way? Or, did something trigger the habit? What would the old you think of you now? What would your higher self say to you? The devil on your shoulder -what could you say to it, whenever it is winning over your higher self?

Change is tough. You are worth it. If you feel like you cannot do it by yourself, even after watching inspiring YouTube videos on the subject, then get help, talk to someone. **For harder drugs, and persistent addictions including self-harm and pain medication, the best thing to do is to get help by contacting a helpline. Tell someone.**

Believe it or not, if you are not ready to quit drugs of any kind, including alcohol, recovery centres will not judge you for this. There is a difference between rehabilitation and recovery centres. The latter can help you to not lose everything, while you are making your choices. They can help make sure your rent is paid, offer food vouchers, support with your power bills, work with your debts, and ensure that you are as safe as you possibly can be, while you are still using. Eventually, you can come to your decision for change in your own time. They are there for you, and they understand how difficult your journey is. They can support families of those with additions too.

ALTERNATIVES

Try replacing:
- A glass of wine with fruit juice with ice
- Cutting yourself with pinging an elastic band on your wrist
- A cigarette with a cup of tea in the sunshine
- Pothead friends with gym buddies
- Chatting online with playing a board game with your kids.

LIMITS

try placing limits to aid the start of a reduction to quit (any is too much but as an example):

- Only smoke 5 cigarettes in a day and keep track,
- Only have marijuana at a weekend
- Have one bar of chocolate a day

BARRIERS

In addition, you could try placing barriers to the activity in question:

- Only smoke outside
- Only drink with company
- Turn off phone notifications
- Don't have chocolate stored at home.

If you cannot do it alone, seek help.

You are not the first and won't be the last.

6

Loss and Endings

Loss

The power of loss is unimaginable. We never truly get over it, it just becomes part of who we are. We eventually embrace the absence and sometimes cope by still talking to the person as if they are still with us.

There is no specific pathway of grief. Even with the theories and diagrams, it is not straight forward.

Some of us become incredibly spiritual and seek out otherworldly modalities and alternative therapies to help us bring some comfort and clarity. Others do not have such beliefs. There is no right way to deal with things.

In a recent time of loss, I was close to a person before their passing, and I took the time to feel the feelings and breathe through the tough emotions. I initially journaled new conversations between us. It helped me to cope with the devastating feelings. When under times of stress, I write poetry and practice breathing exercises, watch mindless TV shows, re-watching familiar shows repeatedly, and listening to music both to connect and distract from the memories. Although even I did not want to believe this at first, I knew this would fade in time to make way for new activities, as I relied less and less on these coping mechanisms and new experiences kicked in. I wanted nothing else than to be in the space of grieving, operating on autopilot and trying to make sense of it all, and that was okay.

Life will never be the same again, my entire world has shifted, and my priorities are very different. All of a sudden, so many things have became clear. I had changed in the blink of an eye. The clarity was very useful in moving forwards.

The depth of emotional pain can cause physical symptoms of trauma. These are temporary and will pass. The feelings will come in waves. Allow these feelings, do not fight them. Pain is fear leaving the body. The fear of a life without your person can be horrific. Do not be afraid. You are absolutely meant to be here right now. Everything is as it is supposed to be -in all its pain and imperfection. The path of life is never without pain and sadness; we are here to learn, to serve our soul's purpose - to serve others in some way.

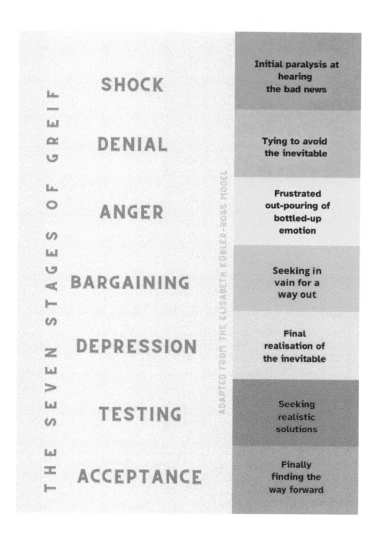

THE SEVEN STAGES OF GREIF

ADAPTED FROM THE ELISABETH KÜBLER-ROSS MODEL

SHOCK	Initial paralysis at hearing the bad news
DENIAL	Tying to avoid the inevitable
ANGER	Frustrated out-pouring of bottled-up emotion
BARGAINING	Seeking in vain for a way out
DEPRESSION	Final realisation of the inevitable
TESTING	Seeking realistic solutions
ACCEPTANCE	Finally finding the way forward

There is nobody out there who can feel what you are feeling. Sometimes you reach out and your feelings can be minimised by others: "You hardly knew him," or, "death is part of life." These are not meant to be unkind. They are said because others do not wish for you to be sad. Most people are more switched on and will say that they are sorry for your loss.

Do not judge others for the way they grieve. Grief is a very personal space. Allow each other to experience and own your respective grief. I wrote the poem, Abject Clarity (page 40), to try to put into words, some of the terrible feelings that I was experiencing during a time of loss.

ABJECT CLARITY

An injection of piercing intuition straight to the heart, like a dagger.

As the stomach twists away so that you'd rather stab it or rip it out than feel the depth of despair. It is the rock that sits and will not roll away.

While the light now glares upon everything crystal, nothing else matters.

The floating stillness, the ordinance, the quietening of the mind, like a padded cell or suffocating pillow on the life you knew before.

The screams you need to let out as roars, like rescinding birth.

The silence of the phone, the arms that will never be around you, the touch that would electrify your soul is extinguished.

This is now, forever part of my soul as long as the clock ticks in the cosmic caverns of time.

SUICIDAL THOUGHTS?

Everything external can be sorted. Pressures can be removed and there is always someone who can help. Please keep reaching out. There is always another way out. Even of you cannot see it, even if you are in a dark void, unable to breathe. This too shall pass. Do not take the action. I have lost people to suicide. I would invite anyone with these thoughts to seek help. Please call a helpline to talk it through.

Feeling invisible and worthless, can lead to self-harm and suicidal thoughts, even hearing voices. Remember this... **ALL FEELINGS ARE TEMPORARY.**

If you experience any of these feelings, tell someone, call a helpline, and do not delay in doing so. There are people to assist you without judgement. Instead of "why me?" go for "try me!" and keep going. You are a warrior. A phrase I hear often is, "God only gives you what you can cope with." I sometimes switch this out for, "The universe only gives you what you can cope with." Whatever suits you to say. You are 100% meant to come through this time in your life, and emerge stronger afterwards.

You can get through this, and you can cope. You have got through 100% of your bad days so far. Call a helpline and deal with those feelings. It can take all of your strength to battle those demons. You are absolutely not alone in this world. **YOU ARE NOT ALONE.**

If you have lost someone to suicide, this is not your fault. Your journey is not over, so work on that as you work through your loss. You can and will get through this.

Endings

I would be as bold as to say that when a relationship ends, no matter what the reason, we grieve. You can tell yourself whatever you like, and make out to all your friends that this is brilliant. Long term, it probably is, however you still need to process the ending. You may have gone through all seven stages of grief while still in the relationship, and gone around it in circles several times before leaving (See the abuse cycle). So, when you leave, you sleep it off and then you might feel like you have been let out! Be careful at this point because you will be quite raw for a long time, and could be vulnerable to rebound relationships. You will grieve for having someone to sleep next to you at night, you will have the good times and bad times go around in your head. Learn to be you again; it takes time. (Also see page 51.)

You may have been the one who was left. Keep your dignity. Maybe it is best not to call/text him/her/them; keep it business if you have to. Let it go. Justice is universal. Karma, the universe, whatever you believe in, will deal with this and you will not have to. You need to focus on you and your healing. Go to friends, family, a therapist. The person who left you is none of these things. Abandonment is an awful feeling. As much as that emptiness and pain claws away at your insides and burns your eyes, let them go. If you need to keep it amicable, do so. Ideally, keep emotion out of it. Focus on your own emotional healing. Keep a journal; write emails to yourself as if it is to them. Your silence is the best 'punishment' if that is what you want to make it feel like. The best 'revenge' is getting on with your life as a strong, independent person. You need not justify anything to the person who let you down.

You may be ending something about yourself, in or out of a relationship. Be strong in your beliefs and don't let anyone hold you back. Stay positive. You can achieve anything you put your mind to. If you are in a relationship with difficulties, two people who love each other and want to make things work, can do so. I still believe that couples therapy can help if you are struggling with communication. You both get to listen to each other and work on things.

Sometimes you just have to let someone go for the sake of your own sanity. This is always difficult, full of mixed emotions. You have to do the right thing for yourself. If you are not functionng, you cannot help anyone else.

"Time wounds all heels." - Marshall Reid

Things end. We lose those that we love. Death is a certainty of life. Being left behind is extremely hard. Even if a passing of a loved one is expected, there are emotions associated with the emptiness, particularly if you have been a carer. It can seem that your entire role in life has gone. I refer back to page 21; there are no unthinkable thoughts and no unfeelable feelings.

The seven stages of grief are not necessarily linear. Sometimes we can experience two at once, skip a stage and go back to it, or spend a long time in one stage. All of this is okay. This will eventually move forward. It takes a long time. For some it never goes away, it just gets less difficult to deal with through the years. The first year after a loss is always the hardest, I have heard. First birthday, Christmas, summer etc. Losing someone suddenly and unexpectedly can bring immense trauma. The chapter on when time stands still, is a guide of how to begin to cope. There is nothing straight forward and no rule book. You are not alone. You can reach out to a bereavement therapist. I remember when my friend lost her husband suddenly. For an entire year, I was at the end of the phone, day and night.

The Art of Starting Again, implies there has been some sort of ending. It could be that you are literally grieving for the passing of someone close to you, therefore you are working on rebuilding after that. Death can feel like a type of abandonment.

It can hurt so much that making sense of these feelings may never be fully achieved. We get to learn to live with that.

If—

BY RUDYARD KIPLING

If you can keep your head when all about you
Are losing theirs and blaming it on you,
If you can trust yourself when all men doubt you,
But make allowance for their doubting too;
If you can wait and not be tired by waiting,
Or being lied about, don't deal in lies,
Or being hated, don't give way to hating,
And yet don't look too good, nor talk too wise:

If you can dream—and not make dreams your master;
If you can think—and not make thoughts your aim;
If you can meet with Triumph and Disaster
And treat those two impostors just the same;
If you can bear to hear the truth you've spoken
Twisted by knaves to make a trap for fools,
Or watch the things you gave your life to, broken,
And stoop and build 'em up with worn-out tools:

If you can make one heap of all your winnings
And risk it on one turn of pitch-and-toss,
And lose, and start again at your beginnings
And never breathe a word about your loss;
If you can force your heart and nerve and sinew
To serve your turn long after they are gone,
And so hold on when there is nothing in you
Except the Will which says to them: 'Hold on!'

If you can talk with crowds and keep your virtue,
Or walk with Kings—nor lose the common touch,
If neither foes nor loving friends can hurt you,
If all men count with you, but none too much;
If you can fill the unforgiving minute
With sixty seconds' worth of distance run,
Yours is the Earth and everything that's in it,
And—which is more—you'll be a Man, my son!

Source: A Choice of Kipling's Verse (1943)

7

Domestic Abuse

As a survivor of domestic abuse, I have an ever-maintaining drama reduction policy, in order to avoid or remove unnecessary stress and chaos – thus, taking control of my life. This can be very difficult with emotions involved. It has been mistaken for running away from problems. I might call it 'cutting the problems dead in their tracks.' Running away is not always the right path, as it can cause other problems. Changing your environment to enable positive change can also be a good thing.

Lifting the veil on domestic abuse can be a long journey. The perpetrator has often rounded up the troops, to isolate you from support, and will continue to try to dim your bright light in whatever way possible. Others, who do not understand, may unintentionally disempower you. Believe in yourself. Even surrounded by experts, survivors are still being overlooked. I am blessed that I have been able to assist numerous people in escaping and getting their power back at various stages of their journey.

Unfortunately, it takes a lot of strategy to get through the chaos and remaining issues, once a relationship is over. Your voice deserves to be heard and your emotions deserve to be treated with respect. This does not always happen. The worst culprits seem to be family court professionals and social workers for family services. There are some amazing individuals in these organisations, who go above and beyond - really grasping the situation. Then there are the others. Despite extensive training, many of these professionals are inexperienced with domestic abuse. They see squabbling parents on a daily basis, and overlook some tell-tale signs of abuse, parental alienation and coercion in favour of "the rights of the child," as in, the right of the child to not be caught in the middle of parents who disagree. Domestic abuse is not people disagreeing. It is one person, disempowering another. It can take a lot of evidence, and challenge to find the right pair of ears.

Organisations like Women's Aid are experts, and can support you. Police are getting better in dealing with cases of domestic abuse. These are the key people to establish your chain of evidence of domestic abuse for family court matters.

Build Up

Breakdown in communication.
As we know what is coming, we work hard to deescalate situations by pleasing or trying to deal with issues raised by the abuser. Placating.

Percieved Harmony

Go back to 'happy families,' It was just a blip, it doesn't happen all the time. This time it will work.out. I know they are not well/didn't mean it. This is the biggest denial phase. 'The honeymoon.'

Drama

The incident or explosion in temper by the abuser. Verbal, physical or emotional abuse. Anger, blame, arguing, threats or intimidation.

Could you be stuck in the spin-cycle of abuse?

It can be a dizzying feeling, constantly like the rug is being pulled from under you. Once you recognise this cycle, it is easier to decide to end this turmoil.

Head Fuck

Often referred to as the 'reconciliation.' Maybe you both want it to all go away and go back to normal. Abuser might apologise and make excuses, minimise or blame victim.

The Abuse Cycle

Domestic abuse can take many forms, and is invariably about power and control. Aside from physical abuse - from pushing, shoving, and hitting, to sexual abuse, and grievous harm - it can be any or several of these things:

• Coercion and threats – Making somebody do something, like drop charges for example, or something illegal, threatening to leave, or commit suicide, threatening to report him/her to welfare.

• Intimidation – Looks, actions, gestures, smashing things, abusing pets, displaying weapons.

• Emotional abuse – Putting him/her down, calling them names, making them feel guilty, crazy-making, making them feel bad about themselves, humiliating them, playing mind games.

• Economic abuse – Making partner ask for money, giving him/her an allowance, preventing them from keeping a job, not letting him/her know about or have access to family income, taking their money.

• Domination – Known by some organisations as 'Using Male Privilege.' He might treat her like a servant "a woman's job" or act like the Master of the Castle, defining men's and women's roles and making all the big decisions. I think this works both ways.

• Isolation – Controlling what partner does, who they see, what they read, where she goes, whom they talk to, and limits outside involvement. Uses jealousy as justification.

• Using children – Making him/her feel guilty about the children, using children to relay messages, using visitation to harass the ex-partner, threatening to take the children.

• Minimising, denying, and blaming – Making light of the abuse and not taking partner's concerns about it seriously, saying the abuse didn't happen, shifting responsibility for abusive behaviour, saying he/she caused the abuse.

The diagram on page 46-47 is my take on the spin cycle of abuse I have been around in over and over again. The great thing is that, once you recognise that you are in the cycle - in time, when you know you have had a 'gutful,' – eventually, you can take steps to get out.

There is always a way out. It can take strategy, cunning and effort. Do not be disheartened if your long-thought-out and painful admission falls upon the wrong ears. Research, find the right pair of ears. Very often those closest to you are not the ones who are equipped to spot the abuse or to say the right things.

I have had a lot of dealings with various organisations over the years. If you go back to Maslow's Hierarchy of Needs (p.18-19), being in an abusive relationship means you are either emotionally or physically unsafe, more likely both in the end, as it escalates every time the cycle goes around, and you accept more and more from your abuser. You cannot have a decent social circle, or self-actualise, if you are not safe.

I would add that classic abusers can look good to other people. They are often nice, helpful, and pleasant outside of the home, making it look like the person they live with would be crazy to let them go. These outsiders do not have to live with the nastiness, and you do. Talk to someone outside of your family or friends, talk to an expert organisation - they understand.

People don't tend to change without extensive work on doing so, and if you are in the middle of a long line of exes and future partners, you are not the first, and you will not be the last to have to deal with the same treatment. They may learn a little from your absence, but if you take them back, you are giving permission to end up back where you were in the end.

Men as victims

13.9% of men suffer from domestic abuse and 27% of women according to *Mankind*. There is absolutely no shame in asking for help. There are also organisations that specialise in male victims of domestic abuse. I urge everyone to be a survivor and get support. You are not alone. No abuse is acceptable.

This topic is something that is extremely dear to my heart. I have helped several men and women to sort out their abusive ex-partners. The strongest and fittest of men can succumb to domestic violence and some have taken their own lives due to the inability to face the situation. We need to stop this. Please speak out. If nobody understands, speak out again to someone else. It is not uncommon.

It is absolutely devastating that beautiful big strong men are being emasculated, devalued, threatened, beaten and coerced by narcissistic partners or ex-partners. It may surprise some people to hear that this happens to strongmen and pro-fighters. Talk to someone at your gym or sports club -they may have heard of this happening before.

I believe it comes down to being a bright and loving soul with the correct values of respect for a partner and a desire for peace. It matters not if you are a male or female experiencing abuse, abuse is abuse and it is not on.

This is an exerpt from "Sam's Story" on the *Mankind* website, www.mankind.org.uk

> *"The second time she attacked me, she followed me around the house punching me in the head, hitting me with a pint glass, knocked me to the floor and proceeded to drop her knee into my head repeatedly. It was ferocious and I genuinely feared for me life. I also remember on another occasion she was punching me in the eye when I was driving around a roundabout, so hard that she bruised her knuckles. I was however later in the wrong for causing the bruising. The most shocking attack however, happened on our wedding night. She really beat me, kicking and punching me repeatedly. I remember her digging her nails into my cheek, it felt like she was going to rip my cheek off. I managed to get away and ran down the road in bare feet and my wedding suit. I went back because she was threatening to hang herself with my wedding tie. I later got beaten because the cuts on my face ruined our honeymoon pictures."*

Emotional abuse is where it starts. As we accept more and more from a partner we become desensitised to the abuse and cease to see the woods for the trees. Follow your instincts and keep your head. If something doesn't feel right, reach out. You are not imagining things.

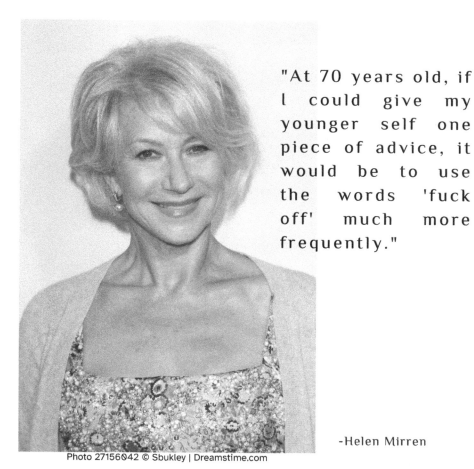

"At 70 years old, if I could give my younger self one piece of advice, it would be to use the words 'fuck off' much more frequently."

-Helen Mirren

Photo 27156042 © Sbukley | Dreamstime.com

It is a difficult task to know when to fight for what you have, and when to leave it behind. "When you have had a gutful," was the phrase one of my marriage guidance counsellors used to describe the point at which you cut off. Invariably, 'the gutful,' takes far too long in my opinion, and if you listen to what your gut tells you in the first place, you needn't get to that level of destruction. Even so, I know what it's like to have to be sure you have given it every shot, before failure.

Very often, the decison to speak out has been long and agonising. If someone speaks to you about abuse, **LISTEN**. It may be the tip of the iceberg.

Helen Mirren is famed for her quote, "At 70 years old, if I could give my younger self one piece of advice, it would be to use the words, 'fuck off,' much more frequently." It sounds rather aggressive and abrupt doesnt it? Sometimes we must set boundaries (page 74) and empower ourselves to speak to those boundaries.

WHEN

TIME

STANDS

STILL

8

When time stands still...

During times of stress and trauma, it is often very difficult to plan anything, manage time well, or set life goals.

No amount of expecting a break-up, or preparing for loss, can account for the level of stress you feel when it happens. For unexpected trauma, you can be left feeling frozen, on autopilot, or simply unable to think, or even breathe well.

You lose time. Sometimes, my bodily functions go into freeze mode, others have the opposite problem.

"This too shall pass." And it will; it can take days, weeks, months; but eventually you will return to a sense of order.

In times like this, my best daily lifesaving strategy is this:

1. **Forgive yourself**
2. **Accept help**
3. **Rest**
4. **Eat something**
5. **Focus on healing**
6. **Do one small thing every day**
7. **Have a bath or shower**
8. **Be aware of what you are saying to others**
9. **Journal and keep lists (you can dispose of these later)**
10. **Focus only on essential appointments and financial obligations**
11. **Preserve your peace**
12. **Avoid addictive or destructive coping strategies**

The key mantra, **"One thing a day, one day at a time,"** will help you survive this change.

1. Forgive yourself

Trauma, freezing, unable to cope, or process what has happened, depression, anxiety, can't poo, can't eat, can't sleep, and any number of equal, opposite, or worse feelings.

If you have been traumatised by abuse, loss, fear, or more, then these reactions are absolutely acceptable.

Whatever you feel you may have contributed to traumatic events, you are likely overthinking this, and you will get to forgive yourself at some point.

You hear terrible stories of tragic accidents, attacks, deaths, and more people than not, feel some sense of sorrow for the people who this happened to. "If only I had locked the door." "If only I had checked my mirrors." "If only I had known."

If time is standing still for you, you are still here. You still have a role to play in this life and you will, one day be able to function and help others.

For now, you must first forgive yourself for all you are thinking and feeling right now.

You are not alone.

If you feel that nobody understands your feelings, you may be right. So, you must consider forgiving them too.

Whatever you are thinking and feeling, it is okay.

Remember:

There are no unthinkable thoughts and no unfeelable feelings"

2. Accept help

This is often a difficult one for people.

If you have a support network of friends, they can help with things like, the school run, shopping, meals, taking notes for you, fencing phone calls.

You might expect that it will upset them to see you sad, shocked or sleeping constantly; or if you keep going into work or the gym, because it keeps you busy. It is in people's nature to say the obvious. "Snap out of it," You need to..."

Whatever is right for you, is what you must do. There are no medals awarded for coping by yourself, working when you should be resting, or having a clean house. If people help you, but offer advice, see it for what it is: Kindness compassion and viewing from their own standpoint. Say, "thank you." Let them say their piece. Say thank you for their care and compassion. Do what you need to do. Sometimes it feels that their help comes at a price. Be mindful of the intention behind the help. It is mostly coming from a place of love. Accept this.

Sometimes helping you is the only gift your friends can give, and by accepting their help, you are also showing them that they are valued by you. Gratitude is always helpful, no matter how low you feel, there will always be something to be thankful for, and no matter how bad your situation: Everything is as it is supposed to be. The reason for it may take years to come to light, but this is your journey.

Accept help from organisations as early as you can. You are never alone, and very often these services are there, with experts built in. Very often these organisations are able to help your family support you. There is absolutely no shame in accepting help.

The shame is in facing things alone.

Remember:
"Those that matter don't mind, and those that mind don't matter."

3. Rest

You heal in your sleep. However, in times of deep stress and trauma, sleep can evade you or consume you unpredictably.

Experts discuss sleep hygiene, stating that the bedroom is for sleep and sex only. Though, most of us get dressed in there too, and a lot of people, especially children and teenagers have a TV in their bedroom.

As an adult, I like to not have a TV in my bedroom because I agree that it is a sacred space, for meditation, rest, switching off, and when I'm in a relationship, I have 'quality time' with my partner.

However, in times of deep stress, having a TV in the bedroom can be a stopgap for when you just cannot switch off. I think back to times when a relationship has ended suddenly, or a major trauma has occurred, a period of 'TV company' in times of darkness can help with coping. I suggest mindless channels or romantic comedies, things that are not arousing or filled with trepidation will help the healing process. When we are vulnerable, in particular, 'we are what we eat,' and that counts for what we see and hear. Weaning off the TV is something you can do, when you do not need distraction from repetitive unwelcome thoughts. These do often pass. Be wary of programs changing in your sleep. If your TV has a timer, to switch itself off, then that is perfect.

Your rest is of paramount importance. You may struggle to sleep at night and so rest in the day might be needed. Time to zone out can be as important and sleep, when sleep is evading you.

Use this opportunity to use an essential oil roller or diffuser. Oils like Lavender, Chamomile and bergamot promote restful sleep.

My doctor once told me that eating a banana, two hours before sleep is beneficial.

When you feel your day is not going well, rest, take a breath and reset. A twenty-minute power-nap or meditation, is a perfect way to reorient your day.

Remember:

"There are no limits on new beginnings."

4. Eat something

When in this period of deep stress, your eating habits may be completely disrupted. Usually, this is in one of two ways or a combination of both:

One is comfort eating and the other is having zero appetite.

Comfort eating can be ok for a few days, but it can become a damaging addiction. Sugar is not your friend and is highly addictive. It provides an instant gratification, but this is short-lived and not a long term solution to your problems. Binge eating can lead to other eating disorders and diseases like diabetes, so always be aware of your food intake, moreover the type of food intake.

Zero appetite is a common symptom of freeze mode. In times of deep trauma, I have been unable to eat or think about food. If this happens for you, ensure you nourish your body with something, little and often. Fruit, vegetables, vitamin supplements, some crackers; -anything that gets nutrition into your body. Try to make it the one thing you do, if it is all you can do, until it becomes a habit.

If your system has a shock, it could mean that you are open to attack from bugs, such as colds, flu, and stomach upsets. Up your vitamin C and maybe take some magnesium supplements or a multivitamin to protect yourself.

Unusual bowel activity, urination, illness, vomiting and pain sensitivity can be caused by stress, these may also impact your appetite.

One thing that I have often done, is revert back to childhood comforts, like soup, and bread, or scrambled egg on toast. These feel like a warm hug, and are no way near the guilt and terror inflicted by eating nine chocolate bars in a row. Guilty!

The only suggestions I have are to:

- Eat little and often
- Consider taking wellness supplements
- Avoid sugar within reason
- Ensure you are consuming fruit and vegetables

Remember:

"A sleep is as good as a feast."

5. Focus on healing

During this difficult time, you may be experiencing so many emotions, or simply feel dead inside. Some of the seven stages of grief may appear (page38):

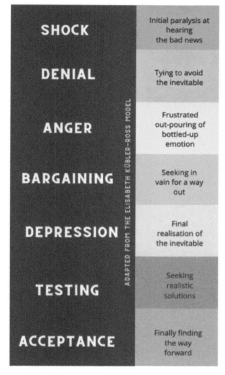

SHOCK	Initial paralysis at hearing the bad news	
DENIAL	Tying to avoid the inevitable	
ANGER	Frustrated out-pouring of bottled-up emotion	
BARGAINING	Seeking in vain for a way out	
DEPRESSION	Final realisation of the inevitable	
TESTING	Seeking realistic solutions	
ACCEPTANCE	Finally finding the way forward	

Whatever you are feeling, it is O.K. to feel those emotions. Allow the tears, allow the anger, allow the 'what ifs.' Let them pass over you as they need to.

You cannot heal or process if you push all these feelings away, even if they burn, sit with it. There are a lot of healing strategies throughout this book, so keep reading!

I have many phrases that come to mind when I am feeling pressured.

"One thing, one day at a time."

"The mess will still be there when I wake up."

"The world will not end if I do not... (insert chore)."

Nothing is more important than your sanity. The world will still be waiting for you to be ready. Let them wait a while. It is not every day that we lose a loved one, or we are left alone or abused by the one person we were meant to trust, or someone is given terrible news. It is important that we take the time to acknowledge the thing that has driven us to feel this way.

Sometimes, in the immediate aftermath, we have some kind of superpower, a way of functioning that is beyond what we would expect. Like adrenaline, nature has given us a gift to flow through a little time before we drop. Allow it, but then allow yourself the time to heal when this fades. Use this time of intuitive clarity, to recognise what is important to you, though refrain from acting upon it in haste.

Remember:

"Nothing is more important than your sanity."

6. Do one small thing every day

When you simply cannot function to pay your bills, see through all the form-filling or official jargon, just stop. Brain fog is a major feature of stress. This is okay.

One day you can make a to-do list, one day you can journal, one day you can face having a bath or shower, another day, you can face a trip to the store. If this is your only one thing, that is O.K. Before you know it, you can do two or three things, or more in a day, once you build up your confidence. Just reset yourself.

One traumatic event happened to me, and my ability to achieve anything among the fog was seriously impaired. I decided that there are 365 days in a year and if I did one thing a day, I could achieve 365 things off my to-do list.

My to do list consisted of many things. One such thing was that, due to my move, some fines had occurred. One was a speeding fine, and another was that a mistake had happened in a toll-bridge account, my car registration had somehow been removed from the account and I had fifteen counts of crossing a bridge that I had not known about. I only found out about these when serious fines, fees and licence points had been added. This put more significant pressure on my situation. Slowly but surely, I was able to take one small step in a day towards rectifying the situations.

The speeding fine, I managed to reduce, along with the licence points but this required several phone calls, of which, each was my one thing in a day; several applications, including one to have a video hearing and a court appearance online.

The toll fines required me to make two court applications per fine, and several phone calls to the authority involved. The amount due was reduced to the original charge for the toll. All this was at the time when I was dealing with the passing of my father, and recovering from an abusive relationship.

Each one of these issues took about three months to resolve, and they were resolved almost simultaneously. I never gave up and refused to let these things stress me out. It can be done, and you will get through it.

Remember:

"One thing a day, one thing at a time."

7. Have a bath or shower

The soothing effect of water on the body is undisputed. Guaranteed, we generally feel so much better after a good wash, or soak in the bath. Yet, in times of extreme stress, the avoidance of doing so is something that I have suffered from. It has almost become a fear at times.

The icky feeling of getting out of the bath or shower, was a discomfort that I wanted to avoid. The initial 'getting wet' forces commitment to the process, which in a bath can be a couple of hours for me, or in a shower, a good twenty minutes. There was a worry that I might miss a call, or be needed elsewhere, leading to stress while trying to practice self-care. All completely irrational, but very real. I would much rather have been festering and actively avoiding the process, I was procrastinating and being almost frozen with an irrational fear.

We all know this is not "normal behaviour." However, there are no unthinkable thoughts and no unfeelable feelings, so, normal or not, it is what it is. Embrace it, but know that at some point, you have to feel the fear and do it anyway.

Some days I would simply put my hair up and have a five-minute shower, though, it was not worth the investment of the time getting dry *laughs*. Making time for the bath or shower may not happen every day under deep stress. Just know that once you do, the avoidance feels silly, and the feeling afterwards is well worth it. You can make it one of your 'one thing in a day' for one of your days, intermittently, for a while, until it becomes routine again.

Remember:

"Feel the fear, but do it anyway."

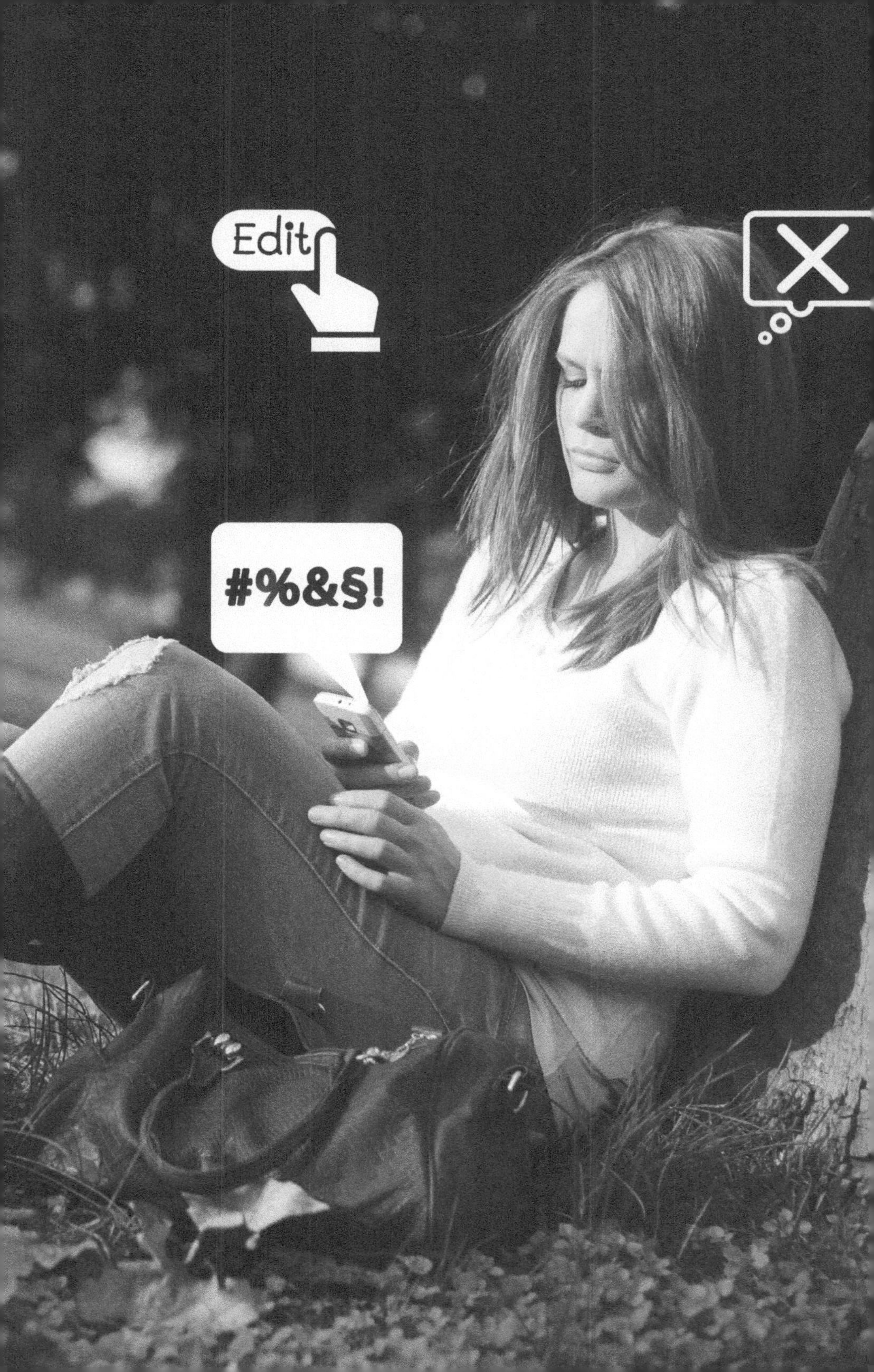
Edit
#%&§!

8. Be aware of what you are saying to others

One of my favourite phrases is, "least said, soonest mended." Your ex is not your therapist, your ex is not your friend. Sadly, friendships can break under heavy burdens and your family will be naturally worried, have what they think is the best advice, and possibly think you are unwell, when you are grieving or dealing with high stress or trauma.

You are guaranteed to be emotional and quite clear about what is annoying, right, wrong or 'has to go.' STOP, take it out on your journal, compose an email or text but DO NOT SEND IT, just save it in the drafts, compose it elsewhere. Sleep on it, everything looks different in the morning. Forgive the unwanted advice from family. It generally comes from a place of love.

You cannot take back paranoid, misunderstood or downright personal texts, emails, answerphone messages, phone calls etc. Even if what you are saying is right, or the whole truth; just stop. It is highly likely that the feelings you are experiencing are something that you can sit with, journal, and expel from your mind with no further implications.

Sending a message when you are emotional can be like lighting a touch paper. Only you may not figure it out until tomorrow, when you have vented, released your emotions, and let it all go. UNTIL people reply, or not, as can happen.

I frequently draft a very long email, copy and paste it into Word, then send possibly about a tenth of it the next day, but worded positively. I have learned to sleep on my emotions with them in a draft. Then I can mindfully edit them.

In life, chaos breeds chaos. It is down to you to diffuse chaos and promote peace in your own life.

Removing all which does not serve your highest good, can be done over time and in a positive and peaceful manner.

Remember:

"Never send a message when you are emotional."

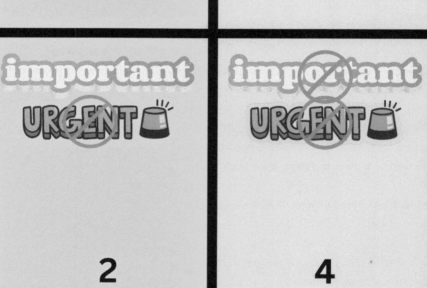

URGENT & important

1

URGENT ~~important~~

3

important URGENT

2

~~important~~ ~~URGENT~~

4

9. Journal and keep lists

When in deep stress, it is sometimes difficult to think at all, never mind **write a list**, or carry out the things on the list. The list can be absolutely overwhelming. And that is okay.

Avoidance of knowing what you need to do is fine up to a point, however when you are trying to sleep, is when it creeps up on you. The solution? Have a notepad next to your bed. Write down the things that are bothering you and then you can tackle the prioritisation in the morning. It gets to a point when everything is important and urgent. Don't fret. You got this.

Do not think of the list as demands, it is not your enemy. The list is a guide. You face what you can, when you can. At this moment in life, I am going through a post trauma response. I am doing one phone call a day and tidying one spot of the house a day. This could be one drawer, one countertop, vacuuming a floor. Every little helps. Your priority is to focus on reducing the feeling of being overwhelmed. So, for me, I am avoiding making anything time-sensitive unless it is literally required by a certain date.

An amazing woman, once said to me, when I was overwhelmed, "Andrea, you have come this far, you can, and you WILL do it." So I say the same here to you. She also gave me a piece of paper to help me prioritise the things that were urgent and important. I have included my version of this on the next page for you to also use. I have since discovered that it is the well-known 'Eisenhower Urgent/Important Principle.'

As per **journaling**, I very often find it helpful to analyse my feelings, and come up with solutions by writing it all down in a notebook. Draw diagrams, use vision boards, write all the horrid, private thoughts down, then draw things into your lists. I usually burn or destroy the notebook when I am ready. The last thing I want, is to end up with someone else reading my private thoughts one day. It is an excellent therapeutic process.

The journal is also an excellent way of dealing with those messages you think to send when you are angry or emotional. Journal them, get them out, and then fish out the pragmatic and positive solutions to the issues you are experiencing. Think of the most positive and polite way that you can communicate those issues, if you still need to.

10. Prioritise essential appointments and financial obligations

If you have managed to prioritise using the *Eisenhower Urgent/Important Principle*, you will have a good idea of what are currently classified as your urgent and important obligations. These are the things you can try to do one of, each day. Some items may take several steps and span weeks to sort out, but one phone call, one form, one letter, one email, at a time, will get you there.

Most companies and organisation will be grateful for your call. They are likely to try to help you by giving you time to process your current situation, and the issue that concerns them. Every step of the way can improve your mood and reduce the sense of being overwhelmed; Thus, improving your self-esteem and self-worth.

Reducing your list to include those essential issues, along with some self-care items, will help immensely. You need to look after your best interests, so helping out at the school fair may be important to you, but it is not going to ruin your life, if you simply have to allow others to make plans to fill your spot at this time. We are all individuals and react differently, so you may still wish to do certain things. However you are feeling, right now, is okay. Listen to your gut, and if you feel heavy when you think of doing something, consider how important it is to your wellbeing and future health. Saying "no," is not a dealbreaker for the most part. Don't lose sleep over it, and have the faith that this phase of feelings will pass.

Communication is key in safeguarding your health, finances, relationships, and family. You do not have to overshare, but you do get the opportunity to be honest, especially with yourself. As mentioned elsewhere in this book, a good friend of mine always used to say, "God only gives you what you can cope with." I use this as a mantra regularly, when times are tough.

Remember:

"Communication is key."

11. Preserve your peace

At times of stress and hardship, we can become incredibly vulnerable to the opinions of others, and the need for human contact. If you are mindful of this fact, you can reserve involving people in your life's business, or even starting a relationship which you may feel is taking away some of the pain. If those people respect you, they will respect your need to space if you ask for it.

This should also be balanced out with accepting help. Identifying those who are helpful can be difficult in such times. Help can come in the form of meals, lifts to places, walks, cups of tea/coffee, and even practical help. Always be aware of what you are giving of yourself. People offering drugs, cigarettes, alcohol, or smooching for sex are often not going to be proactive connections in the future. Try to avoid creating habits that you have to break later. Long-term friends will always mean well. Practice self-awareness and protecting the future you. Be careful who you let into your home and personal space. If you have to stay with family or close friends to support you, do so.

Positive assistance from organisations and charities can be put in place to help people. Reaching out, or getting a friend to reach out on your behalf, is extremely positive. You may not be ready for all of the services on offer. Most professionals know that help is led by the client, so do not be afraid of reaching out and saying that you are not ready for certain things. A simple Google search will bring up a host of local organisations who can be with you on your journey. Sometimes police, doctors and citizens advice services can refer you to helpful organisations.

Believe it or not, the kindness of strangers can be unbelievably positive in tough times. Just be aware of the source of the person. I have received assistance in many forms, and will be eternally grateful for their help. I have also had people taking advantage of my situation. It is always best to not depend on any one person for an extended period of time. Familiarity breeds contempt. Foster your own independence where possible.

"Don't let people upset your balance."

"you can get high on life by practising gratitude and meditation"

12. Avoid addictive or destructive coping strategies

Easier said than done. Trauma can initiate risk-taking behaviours. One of my old phrases was I'm having a spoonful of FUKITOL. This usually led to a night out, a cigarette a drink, calling someone I knew was bad for me.

It is well documented that trauma survivors often find addiction or engage in thrill-seeking activities. I believe this is to control a sensation of being out of control. To feel a whoosh of adrenaline which, in itself, can be addictive.

The need for the thrill of skiing, the excitement of a one-night stand, or stealing, can be masking real problems. This is me speaking from experience of being in the company of a thrill-seeker and finding my own destructive ways of masking my emotions. The only way to heal, is to release the FOMO (fear of missing out), and opt for peace; even when it hurts.

The fear of what our minds will do to us in moments of silence can be what we are avoiding, so we create more chaos. There is no avoiding ourselves eventually.

I can only suggest that if you do not know peace, it is very difficult to identify. At first, yoga, meditation, Tai Chi, and other peace-giving activities may seem very difficult to settle into. If you learned a musical instrument or practiced dance at a time in your life, you will know that practice makes perfect. It doesn't come naturally to everyone. I can promise you that you can get high on life by practising gratitude and meditation, and one day you may have to trust the process.

For me, I tried too many times to move on, mask, and ignore my trauma. This led to more chaos, trauma, and heartache. Peace was scary. Missing out, needing the stimulation of company, parties, and people, all stemmed from having a childhood and early adult life surrounded by friends and family. Realising that you are good company when alone, is extremely empowering.

One of the best things I did for myself on the last round of trauma, was to learn about Reiki healing and how to heal myself.

Remember:

"This too, shall pass."

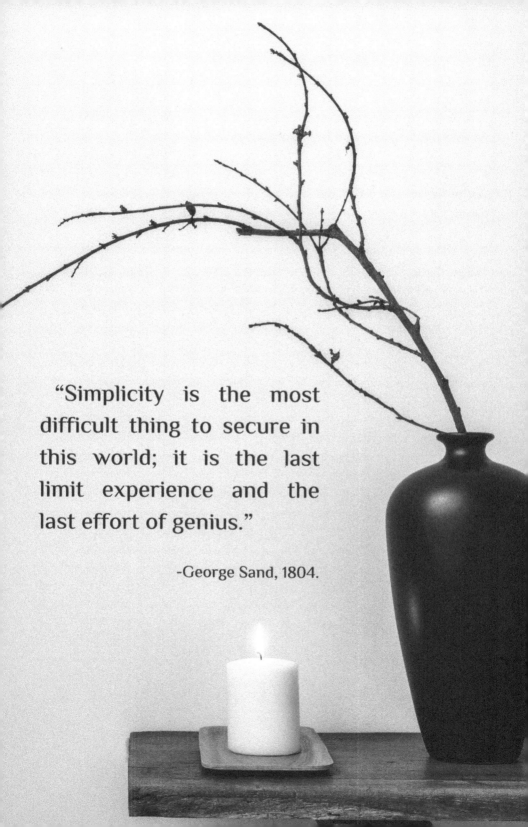

"Simplicity is the most difficult thing to secure in this world; it is the last limit experience and the last effort of genius."

-George Sand, 1804.

9

Congruence and Personal Management

As I attended my counselling course, arriving just on time for the session to start, I could sense that my breathing took ages to settle down, and my thoughts were racing about why I was rushing. There were a million excuses to not be early. The fact remained that I was still in a tizzy. The sense of calm in the room was palpable, and I wanted some of that. The recipe for this level of 'congruence,' seemed to be that everyone else had arrived fifteen to twenty minutes earlier, and had a brew in hand, as they sat on their chairs.

One of the rules of being a therapist, is that you need to have it together before you can help anybody else. Time management, and boundaries, are central to a sense of congruence, and should not just be applied to those who want to become a therapist.

A sense of order can be achieved, by good time management, improved sleep hygiene, healthy nutrition, regular exercise, taking charge of your personal care and health, a healthy sex life, positive interpersonal relationships, hobbies, spiritual growth, proper financial management, a meaningful career, managing responsibilities, mindfulness, and avoiding addiction among other things.

Self Care

ISN'T SELFISH

Holding Trauma

The human body physically responds to stress in many ways. Aside from physiological reactions outlined in the section on *The Window of Tolerance*, our bodies release stress hormones and hold tension. This can lead to long-term pain and chronic illness.

Being mindful, using meditation, performing yoga exercises, and learning to relax in various situations, can alleviate stress, and help reduce health risks associated with stress. I believe many people can avoid certain health problems, -from cancer, diabetes, and strokes, to aches and pains, and dental problems, -by managing stress.

After completing some research on sound vibrations, musical keys, and health, I found many studies concluding that certain musical notes, white noise, and sound vibration frequencies can improve wellbeing on a cellular level. I invite you to find some peace and joy in your life, by taking some time to choose sounds that relax you, check your tension in various muscles, sit with your feelings, take deep breaths, stretch regularly, and relax muscle groups.

A very simple small thing you can try right now:

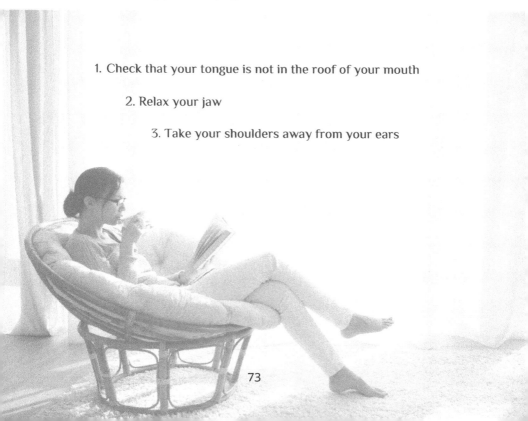

1. Check that your tongue is not in the roof of your mouth

2. Relax your jaw

3. Take your shoulders away from your ears

The people who get upset about you setting boundaries are the one's who benefitted from you having none.

Boundaries

Another 'therapist' concept: setting boundaries. It is up to you what you will accept in your life. A friend would always say to me, "You train people how to treat you." Forget FOMO (fear of missing out), if someone is pushing you to tolerate and accept things that you do not wish to tolerate, or you know are wrong, then you can do without that in your life.

Learn to say "no," learn that being alone is better that being under the thumb. Most of all, have enough gumption and self respect to move on from anything that is beyond your realms of acceptance and skews your moral compass. From my own experience, I know that when somebody knows you will bend and sway, this will continue until there is nothing really left of who you are.

You cannot always put things back in the box. Time might heal wounds but it's best to avoid the battle if you know, deep down, where it leads. The scars will always remain and you can never turn back the clock. Forward is the only direction you are traveling in. Choose the right path for you and keep your boundaries in place.

People respect people with boundaries. What others think of you is none of your business.

Responsibility

Only you are responsible for your life. Things may descend into chaos unexpectedly. You are the one to own the decisions you made to get to where you are now. Go back to boundaries and set them. You are in control; you hold the power. If you don't feel you have the power right now, you do have the power to take steps to gain control. The power lies in your attitude.

A great film to watch is *The Hurricane* starring Denzel Washington. Even when all dignity and freedom was taken from Hurricane, he still had the power of his mind. Believe in the power of your mind.

Somebody once said something to me that changed my life. It was my first meeting with a women's advisor for domestic abuse. I said, "he says everything is my fault and that he loses his temper because of the things I do and say," or words to that effect. She said to me, "aren't you a powerful woman?" It stopped me dead in my train of thought. I never listened to the blame game ever again. I had been empowered.

The road to freedom from that relationship lasted another three years of wavering but I eventually got the message, recognised the patterns and never looked back. When all else fails... remember, "the universe only gives you what you can cope with. And, you will get through this."

Believe in the
power of
your mind.

Relax...

....and let go

Mindful Minutes

Taking some time every day to check on your feelings, sitting with them, taking deep breaths, then thinking of three things you are grateful for, can really turn your life around. Finding the joy among chaos can bring you back to why you are here. I always say, "chaos breeds chaos," so taking ten mindful minutes can bring a sense of congruence into your life and really level you out.

I often find listening to rain sounds, clearing my mind and citing a mantra such as "relax and let go," over and over in my head every time a thought appears can really help. Getting off the merry-go-round for a few minutes every day can see you back into the window of tolerance.

Sometimes, after a period of prolonged stress, this is just not enough, and it could take weeks of finding every spare moment you can to do nothing except practice self-care. Whatever you need to do, do it; especially if people rely on you, as if you are not fit to look after yourself, then how can you be fit to look after anyone else?

You might find that you are forced to take downtime if you get sick, so do what you have to do to stay sane and healthy. Think of the air hostess telling you to apply your own oxygen mask before you apply it to a child. This is not to neglect their needs or prioritise your own desires above those who rely upon you, but to reinforce the principal that you cannot save anybody else when you are responsible for their welfare, but you die in the process of trying.

The 'Things don't change if things don't change' principal applies to prolonged stress. You get to create the opportunity to make a change, in order for things to improve.

"Being kind to yourself only when you think you deserve it, is like watering a plant only when it rains."

-author unknown

Positive Statements

Post-it notes can be extremely useful. I can remember feeling the need to repair my self-esteem. I placed post-it notes all over the house with positive statements like this:

- You are a goddess
- You are worth it
- You are beautiful
- You are intelligent and funny
- You are deserving of love

And many, many others. The walls were filled, and stayed like that until I was ready to take them down.

Transform Your Langauge

The way we speak to ourselves can be transformed by looking at the language we use to work within. There are a few simple phrases that we can eliminate from our external vocabulary, in order to switch our mindset from challenging, to gratitude.

I recently did a course with Mat Shaffer (YouTuber), he eloquently identified and collated several transformational phrases, which I have glimpsed at over the years, in various books, articles, and courses:

- **"I have to/need to..."** can be switched to "I am blessed to/I get to..."

- I always say, **"can't"** means, "won't try." Instead replace "can't," with "I choose not to."

- Own your power by switching, **"this makes me/you make me..."** with "I feel ... when..."

- **"Should,"** is about being attached to an outcome. Instead "I will/I want to.../I commit to..." For other people, "invite them to..." These also work for the word, **"Try."**

- **"I hope,"** can be replaced with "I am excited to be..." in order to become empowering.

- To quote Mat Shaffer, **"'but'** as a mid-sentence transition, invalidates everything that was said before that." If we replace, "but," with, "and," it works better.

- **"Just,"** implies, asking permission and minimising. It can be left out altogether.

- Nothing is, **"unbelievable,"** or, **"too good to be true."** Believe, and accept that you are worthy of your wins.

Tackling Limiting Beliefs

In a 2016 paper by Justin Faerman, of *Flow Consciousness Institute*, entitled, *Mapping the Evolution of Consciousness: A Holistic Framework for Psychospiritual Development*, The *BETDAR Model* was introduced:

> *"BETDAR is an acronym for Beliefs-Emotions-Thoughts-Decisions-Actions-Reality and is a map of the process of how we move from pure awareness (consciousness) at the most fundamental levels, into the actualization of our reality in physical form and our life experience."*

Mat Shaffer (Full Time Purpose) created a YouTube Video, Called, *Hack Your Beliefs for Success TODAY! (Using "BETDAR")*, which explains how to hack this concept in great detail. I have put together the basics for you.

We have a box which represents our beliefs. In order to move the walls of the box, we are invited to shift our thinking. BETDAR, is a six-stage cycle, which feeds our belief system. With the hack, Mat discusses in his video, we can alter our limiting beliefs and expand our reality.

Normally, our reality is created by our actions, our actions are based on a decision, our decisions come from thoughts, our thoughts come from our emotions, which are based on our beliefs, and our reality feeds our beliefs.

Conversely, our beliefs are ingrained in us, by something or someone in our reality, this brings emotion. Emotions feed our thoughts, which feed our decision-making. Our decisions feed our actions and our actions create the reality which we live in, so the cycle continues. This is how we get stuck with limiing beliefs, unless we change something in our reality. This is the *things don't change if things don't change* theory (Chapter 1).

- By choosing a belief that we wish to change, for example, "I am not an author." I am not in alignment with that belief, I wish to change that belief as it is limiting me from writing and publishing a book.

- By flipping the belief, or turning it upside down I am choosing a new belief: "I am an author."

- Skipping the messy emotion and the thought process – or overthinking, I have made a decision. This is the feel the fear and do it anyway, approach.

- By taking consistent, committed, imperfect action with my new belief, I have written this book. (C.C.I.A)

- BOOM! I am now an author.

This is something any one of us can do!

"consistent, committed, imperfect action"

The Starting Point

Working on yourself is no easy task. It can be a truly positive experience. When we are feeling down and the need for change arises, it can be like the pearl produced by the oyster - a beautiful jewel created out of discomfort.

Prevention of drama is always better than cure. When it comes to change management, we cannot make omelettes without breaking eggs; change is usually messy. Some forward planning can assist in smoother transitions.

For so many of us, change is forced upon us, when things are not right. It becomes a damage limitation and reversal exercise. The Universe makes us uncomfortable so that we will move.

There are always barriers to change, even when change is necessary. It is our job to break down those barriers, one by one, step by step. See chapter 8 for some tips on prioritisation under stress.

**Breaking down the barriers
is a daily battle...
Be ready to smash it!
Every day.**

Visualisation

10

Visualisation

Some people call it manifesting. I call it seeing what I want and going for it. Believing it, becoming it, and working as hard as I can to make it happen. Sometimes things are brought our way by us simply picturing it so.

Taking steps to make a brighter future starts with the steps in this book. Whatever I have managed to achieve is because I have broken everything down into steps. My life is not perfect, nothing ever is, but it is my own choice.

You can use design apps and picture collages to help with this. Think of mood boards and wedding planners, storyboards and project management tools with timelines and imagery. Think of one ultimate goal and strategise your way to that.

It may not seem much to anybody else, but my dream home is something like this; a writer's cottage, with enough room for my grown-up children to visit, with a beautiful garden to sit in and enjoy nature. My vision includes a studio for me to create artwork, music, and books in, a space to do yoga and a room with a view, possibly a sea view, to contemplate my blessings.

You can create your own mood board by thinking of things you like. Pinterest is an amazing resource bank. It is great to take the time to do this and enjoy the process. Once you know what you want, your five-year goal can be broken down into smaller targets. Start with what you want and work backwards, until you have a list of what you can do now to move forward.

As a therapeutic life coach, part of my training has been about visualisation. In theory, there is no difference in brain activity, between when we take an action, and when we visualise taking the same action. Energetically, anything is possible. We are all aware of the theory, where what we think, we become, what we imagine, manifests into reality, what we think, we attract. The old phrase "misery loves company,' is the same as chaos breed chaos and peace brings peace. My father's last conversation with me was, "do something that brings you peace. Make a living out of your art." This is what I visualise, daily.

The energy we emit, is priority when visualise a new way of existing. An activity to help change your starting perspective, is to be grateful. Close your eyes and visualise an event that you are grateful for, to change your focus, even using art or mood boards to do this can reinforce gratitude. Visualise the events, feel the feeling as if it is reality. This is the fastest way to create joy.

Some people struggle with visualisation, and feel emotions and bodily sensations rather than imagery. Instead of expecting a visual image or memory, use what you have. Think of the sensations you are having, what can you hear? Whatever is there, pause and seek clarity, colour, or sensations, to bring details to the fore.

We can work to create a vision by bringing out some art materials, paints, magazine cuttings, glue, coloured pencils, clip-art, whatever you would like to use. You may begin with whatever symbols and shapes make you feel happy. Imagine taking your pencil for a walk, you can let your intuition guide the process. make sure you are comfortable. Close your eyes, take three deep breaths. Think of places, nature, colours, symbols and shapes, numbers, words, phrases, intuitive voice. Open the eyes and be ready to create your vision without limits or expectation as to what you will end up with.

You can journal your feelings, things you would like to change, reflect and understand what has been happening in your life. You might get insight for your visualisation in the journaling process. A journal can be empowering in getting clarity for change. Small changes are building blocks for huge transformation. Journaling can allow you to reflect on the leaps you have made. Gratitude is a great thing to include in your journaling to help change your focus, shift your energy, and manifest a brighter beginning. If you shine the light on what is working for you, then your reflections will attract positivity.

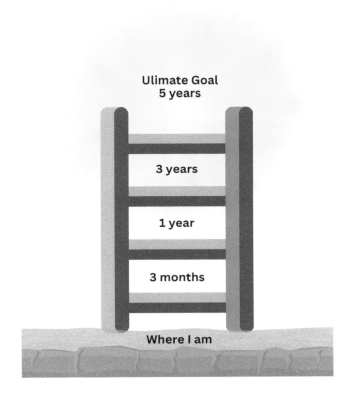

My goal setting strategy employs this idea in each area of life.

You begin by assessing where you are now with your journaling and other techniques, some are included in the next segments of this book.

Then you get to imagine where you would like to be. This goes at the top of the ladder. Then in each rung, you can set a basic example for how far you could get in three years, one year and then in the next three months.

If you focus on enjoying the journey that you are on, rather than the outcome that you are working towards, this whole process can be joyful.

Mood Boards

These are some of my favourite digital tools... (some images are blurred due to copyright.)

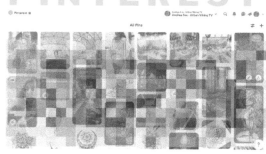

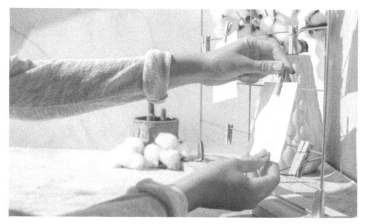

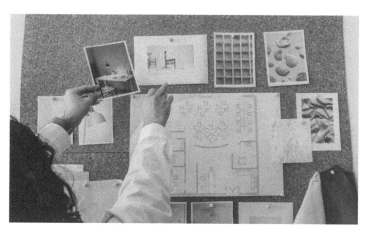

MINIMALISM

DECLUTTER FOR A FRESH START

Mood boards are fantastic for helping with the manifesting and visualisation process. Not limited to professional artists and designers, mood boards allow you to be the architect of your own life.

The *Gumption* scene from *The Holiday*, featuring Kate Winslet and Eli Wallach, discusses how, in a movie, there are leading ladies and best friends. The idea is to be the lead in your own life. A mood board can absolutely empower you to do that. Take the reigns, or at least be a co-pilot.

A simultaneous activity to goal setting, can be decluttering. Minimalism is an excellent foundation for a fresh start. In your visualisation process, it might be an idea to envision all of the junk and baggage that you are carrying around with you, gone.

If it is not serving your highest good, do you really want to keep it around you? Imagine how much better you could breathe without all that is weighing you down.

Mood boards for your life can include a scrap book, digital tools, pin boards, and a visual diary. However you wish to visualise your new beginning, is perfect.

Where I am NOW

I will begin my own transformation with a look at what is bothering me. Where am I going wrong? Like so many of us, I know all the answers or at least where to find them. Taking action and changing habits, are both the barriers and the solutions.

Where am I right now? What am I unhappy with?

At this point in time, I have found myself nurturing bad habits all round. Follow-through on plans is not a strong point when it comes to self-care. Even though I have done all this before, I have found myself back in bad habits. The good thing is that I know what success looks like. I know what it is like not to smoke, to be fit, to be a good weight, to eat well, so I want to feel that way again and never look back.

- I have destructive coping mechanisms
- I feel unfit
- My appearance is deteriorating as I age
- My finances need attention
- I have external pressures
- My home is cluttered

This is the *moan list*. There are positives!!

Example...

- I know that being healthy makes me feel better
- I enjoy eating fruit and vegetables
- I am willing and able to make changes
- I am self-aware
- I know what I have to do
- I know why I want change
- I have tools and strategies to help me
- I have been surrounded by people who are not finding the joy and have made huge changes
- I have been making efforts to get out into nature
- I have discovered ways of bringing myself back to centre
- I am living life on my own terms

Switching Your Mindset - An example

In three to five years I want the direct opposite of all the things I am unhappy with. My next step is to flip all of the things on the *moan list:*

- To have healthy coping habits
- To feel fit
- To improve my image and limit the impact of ageing
- To manage my finances effectively
- To create barriers to external pressures
- To have an uncluttered home.

Looking at this list, I can get very close to all of those if not have smashed them out of the park within a year. One of my major habits to change is to ABC - always be closing, meaning follow through on what I start. This is where the strength lies. It is much easier for me to think, prioritise and 'close,' when I am single. It has been difficult to have partner, after partner who does not see my vision, my worth, or have faith in my goals. Being questioned and sabotaged, is unhelpful and toxic. I am sure that a partner who is truly supportive could accelerate success. I have learned to value my own company.

I can help myself to achieve goals by using C.C.I.A - consistent, committed, imperfect action, flipping limiting beliefs and transforming the language I use:

- I get to change the way I cope with stressful events
- I get to rebuild my fitness
- I get to change my appearance to suit my highest self
- I get to manage my finances well
- I am blessed to have friends who accept healthy boundaries
- I am grateful for the abundance in my home, and my ability to give the things I no longer need, to others who do.

Finding your

There are no excuses, only reasons to do things. It is vital you know why you want this change in your life, so that you can hang on to that reason, and help break down your barriers to success.

My WHYs are simple:

- I want to live longer
- I want to eradicate joyless living
- I want to feel comfort and peace in my life
- I want to be an example to my daughter
- I do not want to take backwards steps, I have come this far.
- I wish to be remembered as the one who never gave up.
-

There are a lot of issues to tackle at once, and this can be overwhelming. By turning each frown upside down (flipping the moan list) and applying some transformational language, then figuring out why I want these things to change, has set the stage for the next phase of setting goals.

I have heard various examples of the WHY. Here are some I thought of:

- Pregnancy
- Becoming a parent
- Upcoming surgery
- Survival
- Elevating your social circle
- To build a business
- A job you want
- A promise you made to someone who has passed away
- A deal or vow to God (or higher power) or yourself as a result of overcoming you may have had no control over

Some things are impermanent. You why must be personal to you and not dependent on the approval of another person. For example:

- To please someone else
- Revenge
- Fear of punishment

These are dependent on the reaction of another person. While these can be excellent motivating factors on your journey, I would argue that these reasons are not going to serve you long-term and may even be unattainable. I invite you to choose reasons to do things that are with your control, and that will help you to become personally elevated.

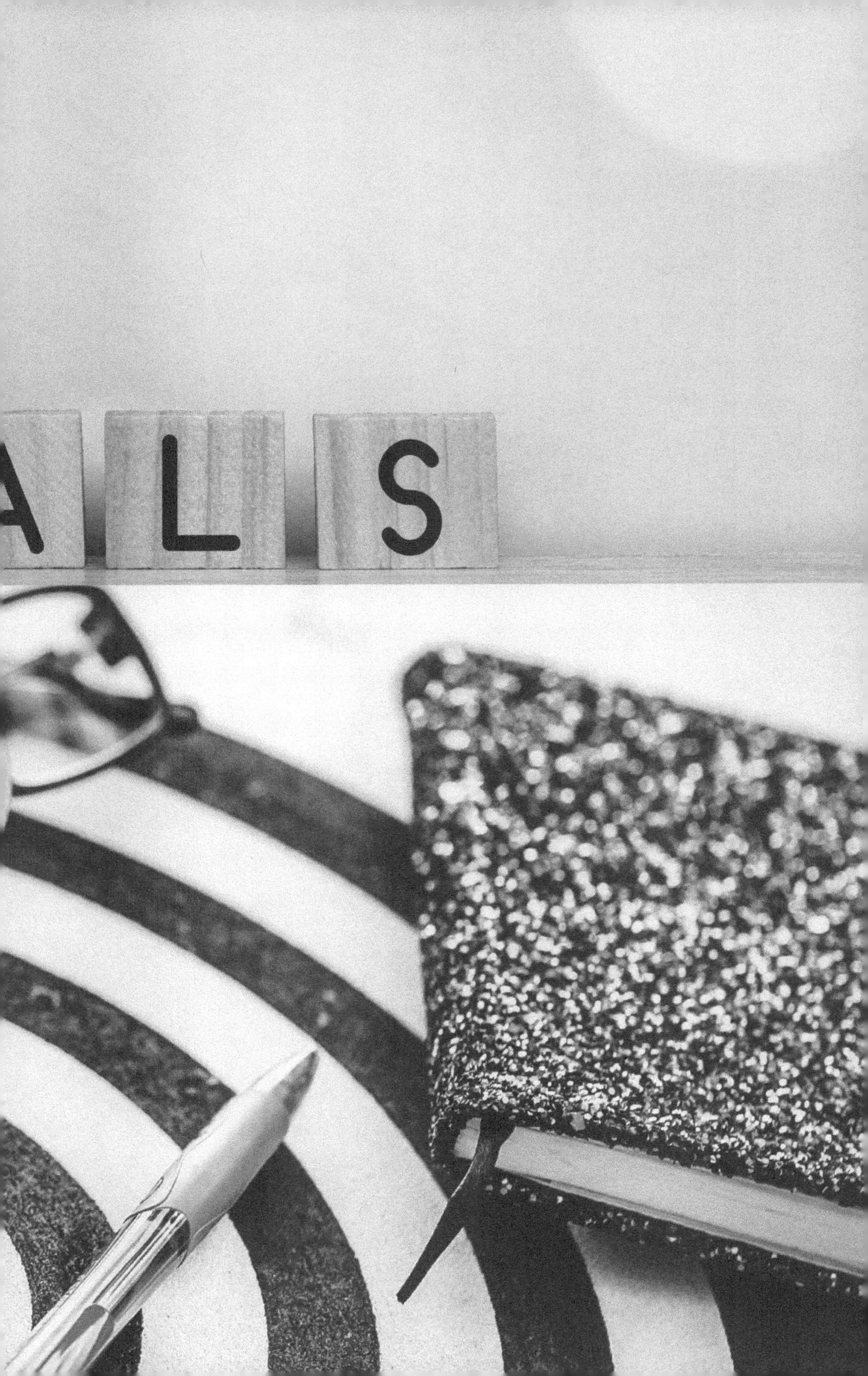
ALS

WHAT INSPIRES YOU?

11

Goal Setting

When it comes to goals, these are consistent, daily choices. Like the alcoholic can never go back to one drink, or they are likely to relapse into bad habits quickly. A person with a peanut allergy, simply avoids peanuts, or they could face severe illness -even death. We can take inspiration from this.

If I could condition myself to believe that sugar is poison, smoking is for sad people, fruit and veg are 'nature's lollies' (that is what I used to call raw carrots for my children), and Yoga is the new sex, then I could talk myself into success.

With any life change, I can talk the talk all I want, but I get to choose whether to walk the walk. This is why finding your WHY is so important.

Some strategies for avoiding relapse are:

- Surrounding yourself with people who align with your goals
- Taking a break to focus on your goals
- Feeding your mind with material related to your goals
- Following groups on social media who align with your goals
- Reading inspiring blogs and watching relevant YouTube videos
- Journaling your progress for accountability
- Planning for success
- Becoming the person you want to be inside and out
- Dressing like the end product
- Letting go of everything that does not serve your highest good
- Decluttering your environment

The RISE

The amount of work you have done internally to set your goals and begin taking action, has been huge. You may have visibly begun to change. Your habits may be changing. You may even be getting some flak from friends and family. Maybe the social media peanut gallery is throwing troll comments your way. Lo and behold, you may even be branded a hypocrite.

In a delicate phase of your transformation, these things may set you back. This is why some of the strategies on page 108 are best put in place early on. So that you have your influences and support network to fall back on. I have heard of staunch atheists becoming church ministers; people who have been making homophobic statements their whole lives, coming out as gay. This kind of turnaround takes immense courage and strength. Strangers may applaud you; your new network will possibly brand you a hero with high praise.

That being said, you are likely to come up against resistance from your nearest and dearest. This is not because they do not like you, or who you have become, who you are, or what you are doing. It is because you no longer fit their image of you. They may be frightened for you. The key factor is that your nearest and dearest, unless they have been party to your innermost thoughts and feelings for the last however many years that you have been considering change, have not been on the journey with you internally. They have literally just got on the train at the last stop when it has already travelled half a lifetime.

Those around you, whom you love, will need to catch up with your new mindset.

You might come across sabotaging behaviours from others. They unwittingly seem to undo your hard work. At the party, you are offered cake... "go on, one slice..." ...."just taste that!" Other people cannot sabotage you... it is your choice. What we need is not a holding pattern, but to learn to say no. Just no. All these people with food allergies and addictions... this is one of them: If I eat that slice of cake, I am going to want another, then before I know it, I'm back off the wagon. No need to be impolite, simply laugh, say thank you, and suggest a realistic alternative, so that your host, friend, or server may still feel useful to you.

The first step to change is acceptance. The decision about what to change comes with accepting things you cannot change and changing the things you can, like The Serenity Prayer. The wisdom to know the difference is also subjective. For example, the people around you are not something you can change, but you can generally change whether you continue to be surrounded by them.

This can be extremely tough when the person who is afraid of your changes the most, is the one you look to for support. Your spouse or best friend may wonder why you need to change. My desire to work in media, write books, sing on stage, and create art, has ended many a relationship. Some people like the idea of you, the look of you, the smell of you, the sex, yet they are missing the love of who you are. They don't want you to change, become unavailable, elevated. They just want you to be the same old you. People fear what they do not know. I had one ex ask me if music publishing was a pyramid scheme. He had no faith in me and thought he was protecting me. Another said, "I will give you a year to make it." Needless to say, I am grateful for their resistance.

Family Life

For those of us with family life, a committed relationship and children, change comes with more challenges. Having external pressure and a cluttered home, financial difficulties, struggling with finding time for yourself, and coping in unhealthy ways, creeps into family life.

Having a family means taking the good with the bad and these feelings come in waves. They are also not just about the immediate family and can be partly due to your own mood cycle. There are no unthinkable thoughts and no unfeelable feelings, however any negative or exhaustive feelings need to be rectified and remedied rather than cut off. Especially when so much fun, laughter, and togetherness comes from having family life.

The simple fact is you get to find the joy. Find the gratitude. If we are grateful, we act grateful, others are receiving gratitude and positivity. In the end, it will come back to you in abundance. Put down the screens, get outside and forget the pressures together for a while. If you cannot do it effectively with your family. Have some 'me' time. I know this is easier said than done.

Out of all of the problems I have identified, after applying *The Serenity Prayer*, I know what I have to do with my positive goals. These are also controlling factors that have needed to be accepted: I am living with people who depend on me, share decision making, and others require my time, so I am going to concentrate on the things I can control and focus on those. There are still minor changes that can be made to accommodate the goals which I have limited control over.

"Poor is the man whose pleasures depend on the permission of another." – Madonna

This quote stuck in my head from being a teenager. Permission may not be what you are asking, perhaps you simply require some understanding and tolerance as you go about your transformation.

Actions speak louder than words, By finding the time, setting your boundaries and taking action, you will find that those around you will adjust. If your changes are small and manageable, taking it step by step will enable your other half to catch up. You can make changes without being indulgent or having an attitude. Being self-aware and mindful of the impact of change can help you move forward. You may get more support than you expected. After all, your family will benefit in the end.

IF YOUR DREAMS
DON'T SCARE YOU,
THEY ARE NOT BIG
ENOUGH

Setting Your Goals

I have worked with this proforma for many years. It centres me and gives me hope for a brighter future.

Health	Wellbeing	Image	Social
Career	Finances	Hobbies	Responsibilities

As a guide you would use these suggestions to fill in under each heading. I find this process therapeutic and the ultimate self-care ritual once in a while.

Health	Wellbeing	Environment	Social
• Nutrition • Exercise • Medical needs • Longevity • Dental	• Mental health • Peace • Spirituality • Self-esteem • Safety • Appearance	• Home upkeep • Home Improvements • Garden • Organisation	• Relationship • Friendships • Eternal family • Sex/intimacy
Career	Finances	Hobbies	Responsibilities
• Job/business • Education • Planning	• Bills • Debts • Pensions • Saving • Investments • Management	• Creativity • Excitement • Sport • Beauty in nature	• Children • Pets • Home • Carer?

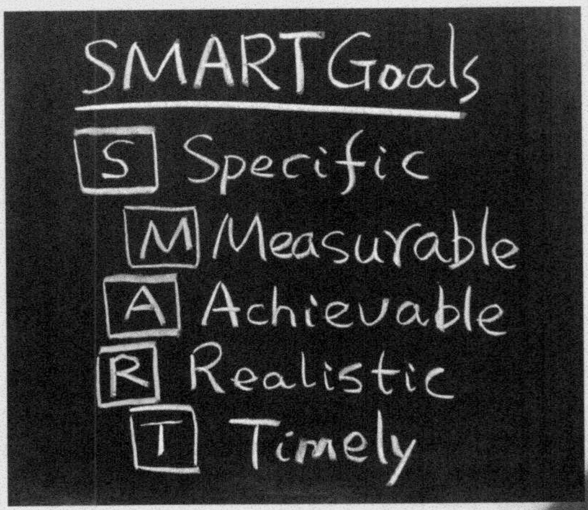

SMART Goals
- [S] Specific
- [M] Measurable
- [A] Achievable
- [R] Realistic
- [T] Timely

ARE YOUR
GOALS SMART?

Meet Jennifer...

To help guide you using the proforma I have imagined the scenario of 'Jennifer.'

Jennifer is thirty-five, married with an 8-year-old daughter, lives in council accommodation and works as a receptionist for a shop fitting company. She used to enjoy rock climbing but doesn't have time. Her first step, as she is feeling a little down is to identify how she is feeling about things. Each window could be an A4 page or just a few words. It is up to you how you do it.

This can be an emotionless process if you look on it from the perspective of a visitor to your life and think what you would think if you popped in on yourself. You are your own worst critic so this is a useful place to begin change.

I find that I am often not willing to sink any lower by the time I get to doing this again and it makes me able to identify what needs fixing, sometimes there can be tears. Not least at the fact that I have taken the step, with intent, to make changes. This tool is helpful in identifying what they are.

Feeling Gratitude

Jennifer writes:

Health	Wellbeing	Environment	Social
poor diet
smoking
overweight
not exercising | don't get a minute's peace
disorganised
constantly tense
look a mess
shabby clothes
nails, hair, skin not looking good.
feel unattractive | Door handles falling off, kitchen tap dripping, bedroom needs painting.

Daughter's room always mess. | communication needs improving in my relationship
not seen friends or family in months |
| **Career** | **Finances** | **Hobbies** | **Responsibilities** |
| not going anywhere, same job 5 years, hum drum | $10,000 debt
want to own house
got no pension | I enjoyed rock climbing but not fit enough to do it now | School runs
Judo club
dentists
walk the dog |

And to turn that frown upside down there are a couple of options to start with.

The first is to redo the exercise using positive statements that begin with...

"I am grateful for..."
"I love it when..."
"I can..."
"I will..."
"I can be..."
"My dream is..."

The grass is not always greener on the other side

An interesting film to watch is *Vicky Christina Barcelona* for an example of how excitement may not be the best thing for a stable life.

Visualisation tips

Ignore any barriers to this process. Have a wild adventure in your mind. Any dream you wish to make happen. Often the reality of those dreams would be overwhelming, or not what you might find you want in the end. For me, a writer's cottage would be ideal, enough money to not have to worry, and not too many things; a simple, comfortable life with time in abundance and people who love me.

A yacht in the Caribbean and a $15M mansion in Beverley Hills might seem out of reach if you are in a Hackney high rise relying on a bicycle. Anything is possible if you make the right sacrifices and decisions in life. Everything comes at a cost, so think about what you want to keep about your life. Sometimes you don't know what you have got until it's gone. Other times, letting go is the freedom you need.

Gratitude
is the key to
Abundance

I think of Levi Roots. He is now worth $45m after he was a successful Dragon's Den entrepreneur with his Reggae Reggae Sauce. Levi still chooses to live in Brixton and keep his roots solid in the neighbourhood. He seems like a very grounded person on this basis.

Looking at the list and simply switching statements for gratitude and positivity looks a bit like this:

Health	Wellbeing	Environment	Social
I can eat healthily, stop smoking and exercise regularly	I can take 10 mindful minutes every day to relax and unwind with peaceful music. I will smarten myself up, file my nails, wash and dry my hair, try moisturise, drink more water and get some tinted body lotion.	I will be organised. I will get the door handles and tap fixed I will paint the bedroom I will train my daughter to keep her room tidy	I will take the time to show gratitude for the good things my husband does. I will visit my friends and family.
Career	**Finances**	**Hobbies**	**Responsibilities**
I am grateful that I have a job. I will train in another skill either at work or make time to do so.	I will seek advice from a financial advisor or citizens advice on how I can best manage to rebuild a credit rating and plan for the future	I will do 30 push-ups ever day and try rock-climbing once a month until I build my strength. Take my daughter and a friend	School runs Judo club dentists walk the dog Take my daughter with me on dog walks more often

It all starts with you. You are the centre of your universe. You are your own supreme being and you hold the power to make these changes. We do not have to 'dream big,' though if you are a strategist, this is certainly possible. Remember, you make your own luck.

We are simply looking at the things that have been bothering you. These are immediate issues that will help you clear some dead wood in life, to feel like you are getting somewhere and have purpose. Most of these things are about identifying habits, changing habits and making life better as it is.

THERE ARE NO EXCUSES

ONLY REASONS
TO GET IT DONE

ASSAULT
FITNESS

How is Jennifer going to cope with all these new things that she feels she now has to do? The truth is, she cannot deal with everything at once. However, she can be doing several things, as plates spinning in the air.

What can she do in five years?
What can she do this year?
What can she achieve in three months?
What can she achieve in a week?
What can she do today?

Looking at the things Jennifer would like to achieve, realistically; these could be the answers:

In five years

Health	Wellbeing	Environment	Social
Smoking is a distant memory Healthy nutrition is daily habit Fit, rockclimbing and enjoy the gym	Enjoy regular, prolonged meditation Regular relaxing holidays Feel good about my appearance	I will be organised. Nice kitchen and outdoor space	Time together with my husband for meals out and the odd night away. family get togethers
Career	**Finances**	**Hobbies**	**Responsibilities**
Accountant Good Salary Working for a company but looking to work from home.	Pension fund started Mortgage on house Debts paid off or managed well.	I will do 30 push-ups ever day and try rock-climbing once a month until I build my strength. Take my daughter and a friend	Daughter more independent Take my daughter with me on dog walks

Visualisation of the goals

On looking into this idea of a brighter future, Jennifer thought about how she could have more money and financial security. Working for a business that works with other businesses, she had seen accountants about the building. Noticing that they never looked short of money, she thought about how she too could move forward financially.

The year before, Jennifer had completed some bookkeeping training as part of her professional development in her job along with other staff members, though she had not yet used the skills. Finding enjoyment in the logic of numbers, she felt that she would like to learn more and even train in accountancy alongside her job so that she could improve prospects for the family. There was even a chance that her boss could be funded for her training or she might be entitled to other assistance.

This five-year-plan, is the first stage in changing her future.

In one year

You could go crazy and add more steps, such as *three years*. This can be very useful to do. For the purposes of the book I am jumping to a year. For example in three years, Jennifer could have qualified as an accountant and have switched jobs, be saving for a house deposit. Bear in mind that some local authorities have right-to-buy schemes with huge discounts, Jennifer being a council tenant would fit the bill in her case, making her goals even more achievable than she first imagined.

Health	Wellbeing	Environment	Social
Smoke Free Healthy nutrition is daily habit Go to the gym 3 x per week	Have a decent family holiday paid off in small amounts through the year. Practice mindfulness every day, even if it is while sat in the car outside Judo club. Have hair and nails done, make an hour or two a week to have a nice bath.	I will be organised. Clear out the kitchen and tidy up the garden, plan a nice outdoor space	Time together with my husband for meals out and the odd night away. family get togethers

Career	Finances	Hobbies	Responsibilities
Apply and get a place on an accountants course part time.	Have a great plan in place for pension and house purchase in the future Have all debts managed well and credit score improving.	I will do 30 push-ups ever day and try rock-climbing once a month. Have built up strength and stamina. First outdoor climb. Take my daughter and a friend	School runs, judo etc Take my daughter with me on dog walks

In three months

Health	Wellbeing	Environment	Social
Finished quit smoking program Follwing a nutrition plan Joined a gym	Have booked a holiday Found a bank of mindfulness activities Have hair and nails done make an hour or two a week for herself to have a nice bath.	I will be organised. Have planned the garden improvement for the year, cleared out the kitchen cupboards and decluttered the house.	Have been out for a few nice meals with husband. arranged a family gathering

Career	Finances	Hobbies	Responsibilities
Have decided upon which course to do.	Have had a meeting with financial advisor and Citizens Advice Bureau Have made a plan to reduce debt and registered for a credit score app.	I will do 30 push-ups ever day and try rock-climbing once a month. Have beed on a couple of indoor climbs Take my daughter and a friend	School runs, judo etc Take my daughter with me on dog walks

It could be useful to break it down to what could be achieved in a month next, particularly if you are working in detail.

This week

Health	Wellbeing	Environment	Social
Have quit smoking plan nailed. Cut out bread, sugar and decreased carb intake. Walk 20 minutes and do push ups. Locate gyms	Sourced holiday agents and websites Choose a mindfulness activity to do for 10 minutes a day Have a long bath and make appointments at beauticians/hairdressers	Write a list of jobs and schedule them in over the next couple of months look at garden planning websites and ideas, mood board. Schedule decluttering of the house and pick one room to start.	Booked a restaurant for a meal for two. Work on saying thank you for something positive every day to those you love with Visit/call a family member/friend.

Career	Finances	Hobbies	Responsibilities
Found accountancy courses.	Make appointments with financial advisor and Citizens Advice Bureau Make a list of debts and find out about credit scores,	Book a climbing session arrange date with daughter's friend.	School runs, judo etc Take my daughter with me on dog walks three times this week.

Today:

This really becomes your daily to-do list. You may not achieve everything in a day on the list. If so, cross off what you have done and carry the others over to tomorrow. The habits are the daily core things to introduce for a true life-change and then you add one or two from the list for the week. Try not to overwhelm yourself but stay focused and positive. In Jennifer's case, an example is below.

Some things are habits and others are tasks,

Habits:

- Limit cigarettes to five a day.
- Make a list of what I eat/drink
- Walk the dog, do 30 push ups
- 10 minutes to be mindful
- Say thank you for something positive
- Take the dog for a walk, invite Carly (daughter)

Choose two tasks from the weekly goals.

On Jennifer's list these include:

• Search for accountancy courses
• Search local gyms
• Search beauticians/hairdressers
• Search Financial advisors
• Call Citizens Advice Bureau
• Search credit score Apps
• List Debts
• Talk to daughter and book Climbing Centre
• Book restaurant
• Call/visit family member

If you feel that all this is too much in a week, choose one or two sections and get used to those changes before introducing another section.

Each day, each week will bring you closer to the ultimate goal.

FOCUS

Focus

I hope I have given you a few tools to begin your new journey, and that my experience has been useful to somebody other than myself. To save one person from domestic abuse, addiction, depression, or harassment from their ex would mean that this book has served its purpose.

To conclude the book, I'd like to share with you a poem I wrote, and to wish you a positive and safe transformation.

namaste

HAVE FOCUS

Deal with what you have,
Instead of what you want,
Forget all that you had,
For all of that is gone.

Never lose sight,
Of what you need to do,
If you can keep your focus,
The faster dreams come true.

Sometimes it gets difficult,
When everything can't get done,
But work with what you've got,
And what you want will come.

be inspired...

Andrea Bibby
The Art of Starting Again

www.urbanviking.tv

The Podcast

www.urbanviking.tv

@urbanvikingwoman
@urbanvikingtv

About the Author

Hailing from Warrington, Cheshire (UK), born in 1974, Andrea spent twelve years living in Australia – nine of those years in Frankston, Victoria. She is currently living in Shetland, on an island about a third of the way to Norway from Scotland. The Mother-of four, graduated from UHI with an MA in Music and the Environment in 2020, and University of Chester with a B.Ed. (hons) in 1998.

A former primary school teacher both in the UK and Australia, Andrea established an interest in writing children's books, and later - music journalism. She became a music artist known as Blind Orb featuring chill-out and downtempo music. Fascinated by Aboriginal Art and the surfer lifestyle of Australia, she was influenced to create visual art pieces related to wellbeing. The combination of Fine Art and writing sparked an interest in graphic design and publishing.

Andrea has had experience as an advocate, supporter, and lay-representative in several legal cases, including cases of domestic abuse for men and women, over a period of eighteen years. A survivor of abuse, she has inside knowledge of the gaps in provision for other survivors. Her ambition is to help people develop the ability to heal and move forward in difficult times.

In recent years, Andrea has enjoyed the tranquillity of Shetland to become an author and artist. She taught Art at a local school and continues to write books for children and adults.

Finding alternative therapies to be crucial to healing from trauma, Andrea has completed training in Aromatherapy, Reiki, Shamanism, Art therapy and Yoga. Being in Shetland has provided the opportunity to be a TV extra in four seasons of the BBC detective series "Shetland."

Milton Keynes UK
Ingram Content Group UK Ltd.
UKHW022200260624
444643UK00008B/111